FIVE - SEVEN - FIVE

I'm Still Alive!

FIVE – SEVEN - FIVE

I'm Still Alive!

And No One Knows
The Reason Why!

by

Charles Joseph Fickey

Bookstand Publishing

www.bookstandpublishing.com

Published by
Bookstand Publishing
Morgan Hill, CA 95037
4061_2

ISBN 978-1-61863-717-8

Printed in the United States of America

ACKNOWLEDGEMENTS

I would like to acknowledge the help of the following persons: My daughter Vera Fickey, who was a TV and screenwriter and a member of the New Canaan, Connecticut Waveny Writers' Group; she was among the first to encourage me to write. Rose Sassanoff, who led the Waveny Writers with much advice and encouragement to all of the participants; there I was introduced to the haiku form of poetry. The moderators, in succession, of The Leisure World of Maryland Writers' Workshop: Mary Boutillier, Ron Davis, Cybele Sieradzki, and Regina Featherston, each of whom conducted the workshop in a very professional manner. I especially want to thank Cybele Sieradzki for editing the relatively rough copies of the more than 1,300 haiku, and formatting the entire collection into this book.

I took a good look
and I thanked my lucky stars:
My friends make good book!

Charles Joseph Fickey
2012

INTRODUCTION

This is a collection of haiku written while I was a member of the following two writers' workshops: Waveny Writers, New Canaan, Connecticut and The Leisure World Writers' Workshop, Silver Spring, Maryland.

What is Haiku

Haiku is a form of poetry that originated in Japan in the 16th Century. It is perhaps the shortest poetry form in the world, with about eight to twelve words in three short lines. Yet this tiny poem can say important things about how we feel about what we see around us.

When Haiku was invented, it was used to express feelings about nature, animals and the seasons at a particular time and place, and to share those feelings with others. So, to write a Haiku means to write about how you feel at a certain moment in time, even if you write it down sometime later.

The original Haiku format consisted of 17 syllables, with the syllables arranged in three lines: 5 – 7 – 5. Subsequently, different forms developed, resulting in different forms. While the Haiku is typically about nature, it *can* be about ordinary activities.

Today in the United States, Haiku has gone the way of free verse and can be merely a short expression of a thought, without holding to any particular format.

I have generally followed the basic Haiku format of 17 syllables in three lines, 5 – 7 – 5. Sometimes, however, it is difficult to start the expression of an idea with only five syllables. Thus I have on occasion taken the liberty of modifying the form to accommodate the subject matter. The subject matter itself retains the same characteristics as those of the rest of the collection.

The haiku in this book cover a wide range of subject matter. Some reflect actual experiences of the author, some are pure fiction, and some are a blend of both. Some are humorous, while others convey compassion. Their content includes philosophical observations about the vagaries of life, imaginary diversions, science fiction, and comments on military life and war.

Time

Time ticks merc'lessly on.
Minutes, Days, Eons.
What will be is was; it's gone.

Horse Sense

Horse stops, asks which way.
I tell him go to the right.
Horse knows best, goes left.

Lost

You find a lost coin.
But you'll never find again
any lost minute.

Advice

Good advice is rare.
It is hard to get, and it's
harder to follow.

Change

Times change, and so do we.
Life ain't what it used to be.
What will the future see?

Twister

Twister passed over my house.
House passed o'er Kansas.
Dorothy, this ain't Kansas no more.

Haiku

Haiku is a way
to say something that's inane
in a profound way

Alarm

Chicken Little said with fright,
"Sky will fall tonight."
Morning came, sun still shone bright.

The Cat's Meow

My cat said, "Meow."
I said, "I don't understand."
…. "Ok!.... I'm hungry!"

Cats and Dogs

"Bow-wow! Wuff! Arf! Yip!"
"Meow!" said the cat. "Dumb dog.
Can't you speak English?"

Wings

New wings. Would they work?
My friend kicked me off the cloud.
Flap, flap! Yes! They work!

Winter

The snow is falling.
Sky and ground; white all around.
Winter is calling.

Crown

Snow falls gently down.
It is now white all around.
Earth wears nature's crown.

Is It

Volcanoes may roar.
Tidal waves sweep over shore.
Earth is evermore.

Lightning

Lightning strikes but once.
Never in the same place again,
says my epitaph.

Life

Days go one by one.
Winter gray's now summer sun.
Life is on the run.

Full Moon

The full moon shone bright
on a snowy winter's night.
A beautiful sight.

Night

A wolf's mournful howl.
The hoot-hoot of the night owl.
Night's creatures will prowl.

Peace

The butterfly settles down.
Sun shines all around.
The world's at peace for now.

A Little Bird

One day on my window sill,
sat a little bird.
He sang songs then flew away.

Home

Home is where the heart is.
So, I'm always home
since my heart's ever with me.

Light

Where light casts its brightest ray
darkness must give way;
Night's followed by each new day,

Please Remember

I have told you many times:
"No early wake up calls."
Why can't you please remember?

Proof

Friends, I fall same as my ball.
I dropped it and jumped.
My friends said, "Yes! He was right."

My Bird Returns

My little bird came again.
He sang songs once more;
then he presented his bill.

Away

When they have all gone away,
what is left to say.
Will there be another day?

What Are We

Some humans are like machines.
Some machines like humans.
Pray tell me, which one are we?

Perfection

I met a perfect person;
never let her go.
You can write the rest yourself.

Animal Kingdom

The Eagles soar; Lions roar.
The milk cow says, “Mooo!”
She is part of nature too.

Life

When you run the race of life,
you need not be first.
It’s enough that you finish.

Tomorrow

What happened to tomorrow?
Today is the tomorrow of yesterday.
Tomorrow has come and gone.

Careful

They told me, “Watch! It’s slip’ry!”
Lying on my back,
“Yes, it’s slip’ry!” I agreed.

Leaf

A leaf flutters down,
the last leaf left from the tree,
its glory's gone now.

Easy

Climbing mountains, swimming streams;
difficult, it always seems.
But not if it's in your dreams.

Castles

I built my castle of sand.
It was my life work.
A wave came, washed it away.

The Game

Our life is like a chess game.
Open, check, mate, end.
But, who's moving the pieces.

Master

Whoever moved the pieces
in my life's chess game
must have been a grand master.

Always

Always, when you think it's through,
somewhere from the blue
comes a tiny light to you.

What Happened

Everything is was,
There's no more is or will be,
What happened to me.

Troubles

My guardian angel
took a leave of absence.
Then troubles began.

Evening

Evening is the end of day.
Toss all your cares away.
Tomorrow is a new day.

Full Moon

Full moon, so big I touched it,
or I thought I did.
Well, I can still look at it.

Journey

I traveled many thousand miles,
then came home again.
But left my heart back somewhere.

Where

How far from here to there?
It depends on where
is here, and where is there,

Delusion

Are we what we think we are?
Is it delusion?
Will we ever know the truth?

Conflict

Life is a battle
between all our inner minds,
good, evil, courage and fear.

Past

Never wish for time to pass.
It goes fast enough.
And what's past is gone; it's lost.

Wish

Be careful what you wish for.
A wish can come true.
It may not be good for you.

Wisdom

Then what is wisdom?
Do you know the answer?
If so, you have it.

How Much

How much is zero plus one?
It looks like one.
How about one plus zero?

Solitaire

If you're playing solitaire,
life's going nowhere,
well, you need to draw a pair.

Why

How fast your life can change.
They're here then they're gone.
Can anyone tell me why?

Universe and Man

I asked, "Who am I?"
and the Universe replied,
"You are man. Nobody."

But then He spoke up.
Don't listen to that nonsense,
man is my image

The Universe spoke,
Look at man, he is a joke;
that is your image?

Then He spoke up again,
You have nothing that can think,
my image does that

The Universe was silent.
It had no answer.
It also was made by Him.

He made everything,
both the Universe and man.
His word is final.

Where

Who were they, the ones we loved?
And where are they now?
Could it be in heaven above?

Far Out

On the way to Mars,
I passed the moon, sun and stars.
Fantastic journey.

Could Be

But for my Guardian Angel,
I wouldn't be here.
I would be up there with him.

Rounded

Twixt plus and minus,
stands a well-rounded creature.
His name is zero.

Happy Days

Snap fingers, clap hands,
sing all the songs with the band.
Oh! Life can be grand.

Clouds

I looked at the clouds.
I thought I saw your face.
They moved; it was gone.

Cloud

A cloud passed by,
darkened the sun, then moved on.
Sun shone bright again.

Life

Is your life so dull
That you feel like a null?
It's yours to make full.

Words

Writing and reading;
or is the other way round?
No matter, it's still words.

Sun

From the blackest depths of night,
comes sun with glory.
Lighting earth's darkest corners.

Insideout

So they died on the outside.
I on the inside.
Which is better; which is worse?

Broken

What continues to function
even when broken?
It's your broken heart, dummy.

Other Side

I went to the other side.
Found things the same.
Why should we expect diff'rence?

Answer

How to answer a question
that has no answer?
There it is; there *is* no answer.

Wax and Wane

I watched the moon wax to full,
a glorious sight.
And then it waned to nothing.

Love

If you seek love true,
do not look in places new.
Tis right here for you.

In Love

You know you're in love,
when your heart pounds, your head spins,
the world's upside down.

Your Name

When that bullet with your name
leaves the gun barrel,
it's time to change position.

Difference

What's on the outside,
and what is on the inside?
Is there a diff'rence?

People

I traveled round the world.
Saw many people.
They all looked the same to me.

Languages

Why so many languages?
Did Babel mean this?
Yes, each has its own beauty,

Man

Is man just a blip
on the large universe screen?
Only time will tell.

Eternity

Asked how long to wait?
He said till eternity.
Why so soon, I asked?

Chatter

Chatter boxes don’t stop;
yhey talk on and on.
But do they say anything?

Travel

Drive a car, take a plane;
even take a train.
Get there however you can.

Speak Up

Like a whisper in a windstorm,
his voice boomed at me.
Couldn't hear a word he said.

Draw

If slow on the draw,
or even quick on the draw,
one of them will die.

Life

Youth is for the young.
Age is for the elderly.
But what is in between?

Reply

If you hurt a babe, it cries.
A child asks why.
An adult, in kind, replies.

Talk

Don't tell me how big you are.
I've heard it before.
You will have to show me.

Opposite

She was black on the outside,
but white on inside.
I was just the opposite.

History

My life history
would fill an enormous book.
But who would read it?

Sounds

If decibels were dollars,
I'd be super rich.
Instead, I am nearly deaf.

Shooting Star

A star flashed through the night sky.
Burned brightly, then died;
humanity's destiny.

Sadness

Sadness and sorrow.
Some happiness borrow.
Maybe tomorrow.

Happiness

If you look for happiness,
you'll never find it.
Just wait and it will find you.

Window

Look into her eyes.
They're the windows to the soul.
Through them you'll know her.

Friend

Who is friend and who is foe?
Do we really know?
What is it that makes it so?

Preference

Black, brunette, redhead, towhead,
Which one do you like?
It is just a hair color.

Stage

All the world's a stage, he said.
And that may be true.
But there are too many clowns.

Crocodile

The croc is an ancient creature.
Here long before us
and probably long after.

Universe

Universe is like a clock.
All things in order.
But meteors can't keep time.

Elusive

Happiness, elusive thing.
Here now, then it's gone.
What can we do to keep it?

Master

"I am the Master,"
said the hunter with the gun.
I grant life or death.

Meeting

Lonely people seeking friends;
eyes meet in passing.
Is this where the story ends?

Ancestor

I looked at the ape standing there.
I asked, "Am I your heir?"
Said, "Lord help me if you are."

Carefree

Children playing in the sand.
Not a single care.
Not long ago we were there.

Fighting

Small children, fighting, crying.
But children grow up.
Now soldiers, fighting, dying.

Age

Fifteen, ‘twas the perfect age.
Life was free, easy.
But then I became sixteen.

Years

On my hundredth birthday,
remembered fifteenth.
Years, tears; wouldn’t change a thing.

Gold

All my life, pursuing gold.
And yes, I found it.
But what’s the good when you’re old.

Up There

“Can you fly?” I asked my friend?
“I don’t know, I’ll try.”
“Thanks,” a voice said from a cloud.

Memory

You never forget
cycling, swimming, or skating.
Lots of scars prove it.

Upbeat

If I feel down and out,
I jump, sing, and shout.
That's what life is all about.

Live

Shoot the works, take it all now.
Get it while you can.
Who knows what tomorrow brings?

Buckle

The Pilot said, "Buckle belts!"
just before we crashed.
OK to unbuckle now.

Diet

I asked the tiger baring teeth,
"White meat or dark?"
He said, "Dark!" and threw me back.

Time

Can we reach the end of time?
Whatever answer,
hurry up and don't be late.

Condensed

Condensed soup and milk.
So how about condensed life?
You just add water.

Fame

Fame is like a rocket flare.
It burns bright and short.
And then it will fade from view.

Money

They say money talks.
I must not know the language.
We're total strangers.

Destination

Sailing on the seas of time –
at destination.
But where and when is it?

Modern Times

Airplane, submarine,
One above and one below,
Auto in between.

Left or Right

I read from the left
And you read from the right side.
We can still be friends.

Dogs and Cats

Cat said to dog,
Why do you hate me so much?
Dog said, I don’t know.

Memories

Memories can be happy
and they can be sad.
We have to take good with bad.

For Sure

The alien came.
How do I know that for sure?
Because he was me.

Happy

Now, are you happy?
If so, tell us the reason.
We’d like to be happy too.

Reality

I was sitting still in church,
my thoughts on things high.
Child’s cry brought me down to earth.

Flying

Flying isn’t hard.
I just got back from a trip.
But my arms are tired.

Drill

The Drill Sergeant barked, “‘Ten’hut,”
all the men snapped to.
“Right Face,” some turned right, some left.

Outlaw

If you disobey
the strict law of gravity,
you’re in for a fall.

Prayers

Saying my prayers I wondered,
I have all I need.
Then what am I asking for.

Searching

If you ever search your soul
You'll find it complex
It is not well organized.

Others

There are those now among us,
From another world.
They know who they are; do we?

All's Well

"Four bells! All's well." said the watch.
Grinding crash, then smash.
The ship had just run aground.

Ache

What's good for an aching heart?
There's no pill for that.
You need to grin and bear it.

Forever

Forever is a long time.
Time can hang heavy,
but not with the right person.

Wager

Do you have a winning hand?
Then sky's the limit.
You can bet the ranch on it.

Thinking

Reading, writing, 'rithmetic.
We all had to learn.
But now computers do it.

Better

Snow storm, rain storm, windstorm, hail.
Bring your umbrella.
Better yet, why not stay home.

Elephant

The big circus came to town.
Elephant got loose.
Just went to store for peanuts.

Daydream

Floating on a summer breeze.
Taking life with ease.
Don't anyone wake me please.

Good Life

It's the good life, they said.
I asked where it was.
But then they gave no answer.

No Hurry

Tomorrow I'll try to do
what I meant to do
the day before yesterday

Stung

Stung by a bee, bad luck.
Stung by fellow man;
now, that is stupidity.

Sharpie

He thought he was a sharpie.
Bested everyone.
Till tough gal got best of him.

One

My wife was one of a kind.
Sew, knit, cook, kids and career.
When she passed, no more left.

Lives

The fireman said, “I save lives.”
Soldier, “I take lives.”
Who is right and who is wrong?

Storm

The dark clouds rolled in;
there was thunder, lightning, rain.
Then sun shone again.

Frog Pond

Big frog, little pond.
He was happy as could be.
Then big pond; sad sack.

Noise

Rooster crowed at dawn.
He would do this every day.
Thanksgiving – no noise.

Problem

An irresistible force.
Immovable object.
Houston, we've got a problem.

Circle

Traveling in a driving snow,
we knew we were lost
when circle became helix.

Road Back

Elephant missing from zoo.
He was found down town.
Couldn't remember road back.

Red and Black

Checkers red and black.
Move them forward, crown and back.
They're still red and black.

Army

"Send men who can shoot, salute,"
said man with four stars.
This is how army was born.

Mess

Rain is nature's gift,
but the muddy mess it makes,
that's gift of the rain.

Care

Bodies lying everywhere.
Who the hell will care?
Leaders must have their warfare.

Glory

In his drawer, medals.
In the closet, uniform
In cemet'ry, cross.

Why

I often wonder why
some will have to die,
so that others may survive.

Poetry

Great poets write great poems.
Would that I could too.
Now content with just Haiku.

Who

Who will see the end of day?
We never ask this.
We always believe it's us.

Sleep

Pity the rich man,
money worries, restless sleep.
Poor man sleeps soundly.

Waste

Sleep, the wealth of health,
which the young always squander
to their later regret.

March

I was waiting for the end
of the march of time.
'Twas an endless procession.

The Music

So time marches on.
When life's music fades away,
what is left for us?

Winter Forest

Snowflakes falling in forest.
Stillness of the night
broken by a falling tree.

Dinosaurus

Dinos roamed millions of years.
How fragile is life.
One meteor struck, all gone.

Unchanged

Dino, roach, skeeter, croc, shark.
Here millions of years
in ever unchanging form.

Shadows

Silent soldiers serve;
and they know well who they are.
We will never know.

Warriors

Warriors all, men bold.
It's for the young, not the old.
For country, not gold.

Ski Trail

Skiing down the mountain side.
A tree up ahead,
Left ski left, right ski right, ouch.

Fill It

"Running low on gas," I said,
"Better stop for fill up."
Sputter…. "Uh-Oh! Too late now."

Pile

Double decker, triple deck!
How high can they go?
Pile 'em on, and let's find out.

Movies

Blow it up and burn it down.
Smash, crash all around.
Is that what makes good movies?

Relax

Holiday, a time to rest.
Pack the car; drive west.
But get back in time for work.

Remember

His helmet lay in the dust.
We found nothing more.
No, not even his dog-tags.

Action

There are too many talkers.
Too many lookers.
What we need are some doers.

Night

Night fell, all was still.
Next morning, sun didn't rise.
Night couldn't get up.

Day

For some, 'twas the longest day.
For others, shortest.
Some saw the end, some didn’t.

Soldiers

Soldiers marching proudly by,
on the way to war.
How many will not return?

Gazelles

Sunny savannah.
Gazelles leaping playfully.
Lion crouches in bush.

Visitor

Back from checking traps.
Sitting on bench by front door,
a large, friendly bear.

Sound

Noise has many names:
music, orating, thunder,
but it is still noise.

Awaken

A tired mother
may sleep through the alarm clock.
Baby's cry wakes her.

Eating

Mother watching baby eat,
Said, "Dear, put the spoon
in your mouth, not in your eye."

Taste

Mother said, "Eat, Dear! It's good."
Baby looked at her.
"Mom, try tasting it yourself."

Food

Junkfood! Healthfood! What to do?
I'd live to hundred,
if I just knew the answer.

Legacy

He wants to be known as the man
who did save Iran
from fearsome neighbor Iraq

Right

The old Sergeant said,
"Soldier, if the paper's right,
everything is right."

Danger

Weapons of mass destruction
are sure to get you,
if bogeyman doesn't first.

Fame

Fame, a fleeting thing;
here today, gone tomorrow.
Why do men seek it?

Reward

Steal five dollars; it's jail.
On the other hand,
steal five billion, a mansion!

Hazard

The jogger rounded the turn
looking up at sky.
In his path, child's wagon.

Consolation

Beside friend's coffin, I said,
Jim, your life was tough.
He said, "No worry, peace here."

Pleasant Journey

We had to bail out.
"No parachute," I stated.
"You'll be first to land."

Totaled

My car was a total wreck.
"Who did this?" I asked
from perch upon a tree limb.

No Moon

Living on the moon
is very unromantic.
No full moon in sky.

Choice

They said you're a star.
I'd rather be a comet.
Buzz the Universe.

Jumper

"How high can you really jump?"
I asked grasshopper.
He jumped. Haven't seen him since.

Howl

On a snowy winter night
deep in a pine wood
The mournful howl of a wolf.

Impact

"But I was only going thirty!"
"Yes, but so was he."
Impact at sixty miles per hour.

Life

Reminiscing on my life,
did I do it right?
Can't do much about it now.

Road

I looked down the autumn road,
Many colored leaves,
Very soon, all would be gone,

Living

A lifetime of much frustration,
living by the rules.
Finally learned, rules are for fools.

Driving

If you sleep while driving
and don't stay alert,
you may not be arriving.

Patterns

Autumn, leaves falling down:
red, orange, yellow, brown;
making patterns on the ground.

Autumn

The autumn leaves ablaze
with many colors.
A chipmunk runs cross a log.

Rules

If you fight a duel,
ten steps then turn; that's the rule.
To live, forget rules.

At Sea

Sailing ships going to sea.
Sailors in rigging.
Circling overhead, seagulls.

Reflection

Look at him in the mirror.
Do you really know?
You better get acquainted.

Last

On his dog tags, letter 'C.'
Sarge said, "Call the Priest."
Father knelt and gave last rites.

Future

Watching the sunset. he hoped
'twould rise tomorrow.
It did so, but he didn't.

Man

Man was left standing alone.
He now reigned supreme.
All the animals were gone.

Another

A parallel Universe.
Must be really there.
Else whose voices do I hear?

Eggs

"Cluck, cluck," said the mother hen.
"I just laid an egg."
"So did I," said the comic.

Age

My little girl asked,
"Dad, stage coaches in your day?"
"Dad's not *that* old, dear."

War and Peace

What is war and what is peace?
Don't ask those who fought;
they do not know the reason.

Grandma's

A white picket fence.
A large front porch with a swing.
That was Grandma's house.

Papa's

One hundred acres.
Large white house in the center.
That was Papa's house.

Search

Looking for an honest man,
I search world in vain;
but don't give up, try again.

Tough

A politician's life is tough.
There's never enough
campaign money in the trough.

Promises

Promises, easy to make
and easy to keep;
but sadly they seldom are.

Stop

If you could, would you
bring time to a complete stop?
Think it over first.

Stair

She stood on the stair.
Had my lifelong dream come true?
I could only stare.

Position

Master of the Universe.
Impressive title.
Position already filled.

Open

Do you feel locked out?
You can open any door;
just need the right key.

Four

Rain, dark, four-way stop.
All four cars started at once.
Four wrecks, no one hurt.

Eagle

High above the world below,
eagle soared for hours,
oblivious to mankind.

Space

So you want your space do you?
Well you can have it.
Just you leave *my* space alone.

Free

Free to roam the sky
floating on oceans of air.
Would that it were I.

Greed

Greed is a cancerous thing.
It starts small, gets big.
It can infect anyone.

Apologize

How do you say, “I’m sorry”?
You want to say it,
but it does stick in your throat.

Book

My life is an open book
read by everyone.
It is not a best seller.

Night

I sat watching the sun set
and the moon rising.
A loon now flew past the moon.

Meeting

We met at a thruway stop;
she northbound, me south.
She's still northbound, me south.

Difference

How do you tell duck from goose?
First you turn them loose.
The duck will quack and goose honk.

Address

Gave Post Office new address.
Forward all mail to
Sea of Sorrow on the moon.

Go

Parachuting is much fun
if, when you are done,
you say, "My body's still one."

Help

Is there such a thing as luck?
I have to believe.
Or it's a guardian angel.
.

Visitor

He came here on a light beam.
No one believed him.
So, "Goodbye!" He left same way.

Change

Born with silver spoon.
Park Ave address; squandered all.
New address: Park Bench.

Siren

I heard the siren.
On the way to aid distress,
or late for lunch?

Phone

Heard my cell phone ring.
I picked it up and answered;
heard the warden speak.

On The Beam

Traveling on a beam of light,
sudden crash landing.
Someone turned off the light beam.

Space

Though he came from outer space,
was a different race,
we still set a dinner place.

Talk

They said the porpoise could talk.
I answered, "No way!"
Porpoise said, "You're a hard sell."

Gamble

"Sin will save the world," they say.
We hear every day:
"Roulette, slots, cards, dice! Choose."

None

Medals for this and for that.
Shadow soldiers none.
But they know well what they did.

Landing

Pilot called, "Bail out!"
He rode the plane to the ground.
Miracle, safe landing.

Thoughts

Being with the family
brings back memories.
Sad and glad, so many thoughts.

Train

On the night train to nowhere.
Finally arrived.
No place to go, no one there.

A-Train

"Take the A-train," the song says.
I did it one day.
Turned out to be one way trip.

Movie

On way home from movie,
met up with fierce cat.
Drew six-shooter, dispatched him.

Back

Conductor called, "No return."
They all climbed aboard.
Train left and never returned.

Silence

The silence was disturbing.
Not a single noise.
Why? He was last man on earth.

Enough

When life seems overwhelming.
you have had enough.
You just have to tune it out.

Stop Light

Waiting for stoplight to change,
whistled favorite song.
Heard same song from next car.

Return

Returned from far away land.
No jungle, no sand.
He decided to go back.

Together

Band played its last song.
Couples left the room slowly,
All with many thoughts.

Express

My next trip to Milky Way,
I'll take the express.
It's much faster than local.

Vacation

The brochure said, Jupiter!
Great Vacation spot.
Lots of room, and it's not hot!

Settled

I spent my whole life traveling
'round the Universe.
Now settled down, small Earth town.

Which

What is smart and what is dumb?
Use those words often.
Do we really use them right?

Entrepreneurs

Lem'nade, kids on corner called.
Expectant faces.
I bought a cup, gave a buck.

Antique

Is your car faded, dented?
It's become a laughing-stock.
Call it an antique.

Right

Does anyone have the right
to terminate a life?
Man, mammal, plant, all living.

The Sniper

The sniper took careful aim,
sighted in target.
Then put his rifle away.

Envelope

He's pushing the envelope.
Astronaut crewman?
No, the clerk at Post Office.

Red

Her copper red hair
was like a glorious sunset
over cute freckled face.

Together

Light brown hair and big brown eyes.
A beautiful face.
Stately figure, intellect.

Dream

Her hair and eyes were jet black.
Her face was milk white.
Perfect figure, and smart too.

Collision

Traveling to the Milky Way,
hit an asteroid.
Hope we're covered by insurance.

Which Way

At the edge of Universe,
wondered, "Where to now?
Round or flat or what? Who knows?"

Good Old

I long for the good old days.
Dime show, theatre.
Nickel streetcar took you there.

Tune

Listening to an old jazz record.
Brought back many thoughts.
Some glad, some sad, none bad.

Going Where

Soldiers marching wearily by,
on the way to die.
Does anyone know why?

Fodder

Let's spare the cannon fodder.
Get rid of horses.
Then no more fodder needed.

Return

I reached end of Universe.
Turned and came back home.
It wasn't there anymore.

Home

My trip to end of Universe.
Five thousand earth years.
Came back home, earth gone.

New

New people on block.
I hear they're Jupiterans.
There goes neighborhood.

Doctor

Lawyer read my will.
Take two tabs, call Doc in morn.
Lawyer picked up phone.

Need

Lawyer said to me,
"You're in big trouble, my boy.
You need magician."

Rowboat

Rowboats are much fun.
But not if you lose both oars.
Then you'll need big hands.

Where

Plane swooped towards barn.
Looked like he would fly through it.
Went in; never out.

Investigation

Got new case to solve.
His last known address, the moon.
No expense account.

Finished

The thief got away.
The police searched high and low.
Chief said, "Make up dead file."

Ball

The football hurtled downfield.
So did all players.
They met en masse; but where's ball?

Left

Pitchers fast ball, mighty heave.
Batter made mighty swing.
Ball left park for who knows where.

Umpire

Umpire took out new ball.
Ball said, "Don't want this mayhem."
Put ball in pocket.

Can

Crumpled can lay in the street.
Magic attraction.
Passing boy gave it a kick.

House

Haunted house, could be?
No one lives there anymore.
But weird noise and lights.

Hawk

Hawk swooped, he picked up rabbit.
She said, "Must feed young."
Hawk swooped back down and dropped her.

Vultures

Vultures circling overhead.
Wait for me to die.
Bad luck, hear cavalry bugles.

Dawn

Daylight, checked watch, ten till five.
Pinched me, still alive.
A thousand shells had missed me.

Alias

I used a different name.
That bullet will be
looking for some other one.

Who Is

Checking out foxholes.
Bill said, "Jim's dead." Jim, "Bill's dead."
Both turned, said, "You're dead."

Moonlight

One night, moonlight fizzled out.
Sent crew to fix it.
They couldn't find it in dark.

Comet

I hitched a ride on a comet.
Express, one way trip.
Said, "Goodbye!" Never came back.

Arrived

Roared through many galaxies.
We finally got There.
I looked and thought, Where is There?

Lost

Lost in the Universe.
How to find way home.
Get on phone, ask directions

Flood

The water rose still higher.
Overflowed levee.
"Man the boats," was the order.

Early

Morning in the countryside.
Grass covered with dew.
Sun beginning to waken.

Game

The rules of the game have changed.
Not the same players.
Why couldn't things stay the same?

Knew

I never really told her.
How much I loved her.
Now, I wonder if she knew.

Queen

If I were a King
with a glorious palace,
She would be my Queen.

Tail

Just when we think that
we've got the world by the tail,
becomes a tiger.

Stop

When the tears have stopped,
that is, if they ever do,
it will still be sad.

Cards

I built my own house of cards.
I used the whole deck.
But it still came tumbling down.

Locked

Yesterday got my cell block.
Minutes on cell phone?
No, room in the state prison.

Gambler

Gambler threw down winning card.
Second Ace of spades.
Took pot, never made the door.

Back

Just back from the front.
He found no cheer at the rear.
Went back to the front.

Girl

She was just a country girl.
Bright, shining face.
Never on TV, so what.

Frost

The morning frost on the ground
said winter's coming;
Squirrel ran by hunting nuts.

Cold

She was cold; gave her my coat.
I was plenty warm
just being near her.

Nobody

I spent my whole life,
just being a nobody.
I'll end it same way.

Somebody

They said, "You *are* somebody."
I asked, "Who am I?"
I never got an answer.

Kids

Kids are nice sometimes.
And sometimes they're not so nice.
But life's better with.

Bolt

Walking out one day,
struck by a bolt from the blue.
No, not lightning; it was you.

Wrong

Will I ever get the chance
to right all my wrongs?
Now, every day I hope so.

Bells

Bells were ringing and ringing.
What kind of bells?
Silver, golden, brass and iron.

Remember

She was unforgettable.
Uh, what was her name?
Sorry, I have forgotten.

Schoolhouse

The schoolhouse burned down.
Not one of the children cried.
Just the moms and dads.

Good Old Days

Recall when all cost nickels.
A buck went long way.
You made a dollar a day.

Gone

The bluebird of happiness:
last seen going south,
and he has never returned.

Plan

The mist in the morn.
The new day now being born.
It's nature at work.

Stolen

I stole an idea.
It's when I said, "I love you."
That's been said before.

You

Yes, the very thought of you
sends me to the clouds.
And it takes long to come down.

Enemy

I am fighting the enemy.
Who are they today?
Know who they were yesterday.

Friends

So, as enemies we fought.
When peace declared,
we became the best of friends.

Parallel

Ride through black hole was rough.
Came out on other side.
Right, left, up, down all reversed.

Long Trip

Neptune used to be long trip.
But not anymore.
Ioncruisers get there fast.

Galaxy

Oh galaxy, schmalaxy.
Don't fiddle around.
Let's take a long trip this time.

Space Dozer

Dozing off in outer space,
Galaxer woke up.
Oops, overshot Milky Way.

End

I followed the Milky Way
'til it came to end.
I turned left into black hole.

Burger

At the Burger King.
I ordered dollar special.
Ate it, and another.

Sound

Too much noise is bad.
Too much silence is worse.
Look for happy medium.

Dusk

Crickets were chirping
and the fireflies were blinking.
A bat flew weirdly by.

Lunar

They say I'm a lunatic
and they may be right.
I act weird by full moon.

Boat

High noon, bright sun shone on harbor.
Morn fog mostly gone.
A small tug chugged noisily by.

Arithmetic

Once knew five people.
First one left, then another.
Now that makes three left.

The Best

Five bucks for a cup of coffee,
the panhandler begged,
standing in front of Starbucks

Movie

“May I have a dime?”
I asked my Grandpa one day.
There’s a good movie.

Ending

Darkness slowly descending.
The day was ending.
Full moon peeked over the hills.

Schedule

I missed early bus to the moon.
But not to worry;
there'll be another later.

Morning

"May I come in folks?"
said the bright sun one morning.
Welcome mat was out.

Climber

The morning glory climbed up.
Peeked into my window,
Followed by small humming bird.

Gunslingers

Walked slowly towards each other.
Each with gun slung low.
They embraced, were best of friends.

Noon

High noon came and went
It was really non-event.
Clouds obscured the sun.

Car

Big car tooted, sped past me.
Two miles further,
saw big car off road in ditch.

Turn

Hairpin turn at fifty-five.
Am I still alive?
Someone turned that wheel for me!

Close

Had to pass parked car on curve.
Saw approaching car.
Squeezed by, shook hands in passing.

Status

There was a big explosion.
Stood there, and voice said,
Go sign your death certificate.

Looks

Ape said to monkey,
"You're a homely little twerp."
Monk said, "Look in mirror."

Eruption

Fire rained down from the skies.
Hot and flowing rocks.
Reaction from living earth.

You

Long, long before time began.
Small amoebae formed.
It grew and grew, into you.

Visitors

It was supper time for kids.
A large crowd marched in.
Mom, these are the starving kids.

Last

Drink up pal, it's time to go.
Bartender's warning.
Lonely evening and night.

Work

Doorbell rang; salesman.
"Ma'am! Whiz will do half your work."
She said," Good, take two."

List

"What do you want for Christmas,"
Santa Claus asked her?
She talked till store lights went out.

Soul

Music is food for the soul,
musicians tell us.
But some brings indigestion.

Tree

Only God can make a tree,
so the poem says.
But man can destroy them all.

Different

Day creatures and night creatures
live in different worlds.
But it's really the same world.

Kite

Flying kite at shore.
It was out two thousand feet.
Nearly snared copter.

Day at the Beach

The sandcrab spoke up to me,
Got aquarium?
Those fishing boats are murder.

Seashore

Salt spray blowing in my face.
The tide coming in.
Cries of seagulls overhead.

Visit

Thanksgiving visit to family.
Stay how long you want.
Left day after New Years' day.

Bride

Traveled far and traveled wide.
Looked for blushing bride.
No luck. Girls don’t blush no more.

Modern

What happened to knobs and dials?
So easy to use.
Now we’ve buttons and digits.

Slick

Lots of guts, sped in the rain.
Slick road with sharp turn.
Oops, where did that road go to?

Future

Have you gone digital yet?
Wave of the future.
No dials, lots of numbers.

Advance

Cannons roared and bugles blew.
Soldiers charged ahead.
Minutes later, many dead.

Him Too

Fired my last shot, fixed bayonet.
Waited for enemy.
Got near, could see eyes scared as mine.

Biker

The biker roared by.
Only vehicle moving
through that traffic jam.

Charge

Horses snorted, bugles blared.
Hooves pounded the turf.
Cavalry charged, sabers swinging.

Lost

Called on galactaphone.
Need help, lost in galaxy.
OK, what's nearest star?

Out

Ball was hit out of the park.
Caught by late player.
Brought in ball; is that an out?

Coffee

"You look tired. Cup of coffee?"
my bunk mate asked.
What I need is coffee shower.

Coke

"Want some coke?" bartender asked.
Expected cola;
got shot in vein, not cola.

It's Great

We can bottle It.
And sell It by the dozen.
It will make money.

Action

Some will think before they act.
Others don't bother.
You can see the difference.

Look Out

Basso perfundo's voice boomed.
Crystal chandelier
began to shake, it was doomed.

Slaughter

"Kill 'em!" the crowd cried.
Roman ampetheatre?
No, just a pro football game.

Prom

Listening to an old swing tune,
I thought of the prom.
Yeah, that's where I met your Mom.

Tin Pan Cab

Stuck with cabbie humming song.
I wrote it all down.
Sold it and we made millions.

What

I was so excited,
waiting for it to happen.
Can you tell me what?

Strumming

Watching the sun going down,
strummed my guitar.
Horse said, "Play something new dude."

Smile

"Smile! It won't hurt you," said sign
on good old Gramp's desk.
Funny thing; he rarely did.

Lonely

Who are the lonely, I asked.
Sadly close to home.
Because they are you and me.

Tron

I live in a computer.
Name is Alec Tron.
You can reach me on the keys.

Compromised

Sniper took aim, shot rang out.
Sniper slumped down dead.
Another sniper fired first.

Speed

Light years were too long and slow;
so designed heavy years.
Greatly cut space travel time.

Umbrella

"Go fix that solar panel,"
said space ship captain.
"Take umbrella. It's raining."

Ambitious

Taught horse to tap Morse code,
so he talks to us.
Now he wants to learn the drums.

No Show

One day, after years
of a perfect attendance,
the sun failed to show

Together

Ahead, saw sun rise.
Then in the rear view mirror,
Saw full moon setting.

Rain

The rain spattered on the leaves
and trickled on down.
Local frog in his glory.

Mister Moon

Said his name is Mister Moon.
Each night my child said,
“Good night, Mister Moon.”

Chick

Pity the poor little chicken.
She lays eggs for us.
What more can we ask from her?

End

Is it the end of the world?
Trouble everywhere.
Why can't we live together?

Hometown

It's just a small mountain town.
But it's my whole world.
Born and spent all my life there.

Baloney

"That is baloney," I said.
"Bologna," he asked?
"No, baloney," I answered.

Hit

It was a homer.
You mean a baseball slam bang?
No! It's a pigeon.

Dance

I saw her across the room.
So, asked her to dance.
It became a lifelong romance.

Daisy

I pulled, “She loves me.”
So said the daisy petals.
Then, “She loves me not.”

Angel

His guardian Angel
must be working overtime
looking out for him.

Dairy

I was raising cows on Mars;
the six legged types –
lots of legs, but not much milk.

Solution

It came in a dream.
What could I do about it?
Woke up, forgot it.

Croc

He was one hundred years old.
You mean your Grandpa?
No; my pet crocodile.

Race

Other car had nitrous boost.
How could I keep up?
Strapped on two Jato rockets.

Shadow

If bothered by a shadow.
there's no problem here.
Just turn out the light, it's gone.

Light

I found a new source of light
It is the light dump.
That's where light goes when turned out.

Goal

Kicked field goal from fifty.
So what's the problem?
He kicked in wrong direction.

Direction

Ran ball in from the fifty.
So why the big groans?
He ran to the wrong goal line.

Worker

Need a hard worker.
Get yourself an elephant;
he works for peanuts.

Geometry

I'm geometrical Joe.
Lines, curves, angles; I know.
Powers, square roots? No.

Home

The visitors said,
My house, walk through memory lane.
That's how I like it.

Knew

We were the shadow soldiers.
None knew who we were.
We didn't know each other.

Black and Red

They called it, "Black" operations.
Should have called it red,
since so many people bled.

Trust

Who can you trust?
Wife, doctor, lawyer, policeman?
I'll bet on the wife.

Confidant

I confided everything.
He told everyone.
My life is now known to all.

Doctor

Went to doctor, "said I'm OK."
Next day, Gabriel said,
"Pal, you had the wrong doctor."

Old Hat

In open plane door, I quipped,
"I been there, done that."
Jumpmaster shoved me; no chute.

Trouble

The Indians were whooping loud.
Arrows were flying.
Where are those Cavalry bugles?

Excitement

The nurse took my blood pressure.
It was up, sky high.
If you saw her, you'd know why.

Hand

Life dealt me a lousy hand.
Played it best I could.
Did pretty well, anyway.

No Pain

Roses and people crying.
Why do they weep?
Pain no more, just sleep.

Friends

Friendly scarecrow in corn field.
Friendly crows perched on him.
A big happy family.

What

She wasn't fat, and not thin.
She wasn't short or tall.
What was she, she wasn't.

Ball

"Where did it go?" asked umpire.
Look for dropping ball.
Balls fell from sky like rain drops.

Caught

I was caught up in the draft.
Military service?
No, it was a hurricane.

Eggs

Cook asked, “Boiled, fried or scrambled?”
Said, “Over easy.”
Flipped pan; two eggs on ceiling.

Double

Inebriated patron,
“You two guys! Give me a drink.”
“We’re one; and it’s no.”

History

Asked class, “You like history?”
Smart aleck replied,
“Don’t know. I’ve never tried it.”

Winner

The battle rages.
TV, film, radio, books.
Who’s winning? Who cares?

Line

The marchers' line stretched for miles.
Footprints in the snow;
captured, headed for prison camp.

Time

Is there real time machine?
Take you back and forth?
Yes! Imagination.

Age

Astronauts age fast.
See many, many suns.
Go backwards, younger.

Birds

Saw many birds flying south.
Is winter coming?
No, 'twas an aviathon.

Kick

Practiced long, kicking dummy.
Then entered contest.
Problem: opponent kicked back.

Money

Saving money is a drag.
Spending is more fun.
Paying bills is the worst.

Curve

Took curve on two wheels.
Was it a speeding auto?
No, a bicycle.

You

On a scale of one to ten,
how happy are you?
You must answer this yourself.

Alone

Alone, my thoughts turned to you.
Not much I can do.
Still thinking, but still alone.

Trip

Took trip half-way round world.
'Twas not far enough.
For you took a longer trip.

Moonlight

The moon was so bright.
Cast your beautiful shadow.
Cloud came, shadow gone.

Nature

So what is nature?
Is man. He must be, because
he is not man made.

Difference

Nature's not man made;
It is divine creation.
That is the difference.

Man

So then what is man?
Is he divine creation?
Or is he man made?

Haiku

Haiku is a poem
Of seventeen syllables
And about nature.

Day

The curtain of night parted
and let the sun in.
A glorious new day started.

Trip

The Sea of Sorrow,
On the moon. Can I go there?
Maybe tomorrow.

Formation

Supernova came to life.
Threw out bolts of fire.
One cooled, became Earth.

Possible

One night I looked at the sky.
Saw the shining Earth.
Can we reach Earth from Moon?

People

Sailing on the Sea of Sorrow.
Looked up at the sky.
What are Earth people like?

Truth

"Is it true?" they asked.
As I told lie after lie.
"Or is it fiction?"

Bluster

It's the scourge of all mankind.
"What is it? I asked
Didn't know, just blustering

Travel

The canals on Mars
make travel free and easy.
That's why they are there.

Name

Poster: Wanted dead or alive.
Brought him dead; no good.
Can't identify himself.

Phase

Life is but one phase
we have in the Universe.
Death is the next phase.

Year

Winter, spring, summer, autumn.
Season follows season.
Another year has gone by.

Journey

Sun climbs the near slope of day.
Passes the day's peak.
Then descends down the far side.

Peace

Quiet, peaceful Universe.
Ast'roids, comets, meteorites.
Hurtling, colliding.

Wish

If I had one wish.
Not gold, youth, eternity.
I'd want my girls back.

Drag

I've nothing to do
and no place to go, time drags.
That's life without you.

Some

Yes, somewhere, someday, someone
will be there for me.
Until then, I'll wait to see.

Meet

Now you went away.
I don't know where, don't know why.
Will we meet again?

Duty

My job is to lie
It's my duty, they pay me
Do you believe this?

Know

Nobody knows me.
That's the way it has to be
for life; forever.

Real

Will the real me stand up?
Well, nobody stood up.
Since there is no real me.

Lie

My life is a lie
in a long continuous stream.
The truth? What is that?

Regs

Army has regulations.
We had our own regs.
That's how we got our job done.

Beat

Lost all that mattered.
My heart and soul were battered.
My whole life shattered.

Name

They gave me new name.
Then they sent me on my way.
Nobody knows where.

World

Goodbye to old world.
It's a whole 'nuther world now.
Liked the old better.

Life

That's all there is to life.
Just a little laughs,
and just a few little tears.

Day

Dawn is start of new day.
Twilight is the end of day.
In between is yours.

End

'Twas solar pulse
that destroyed dinosaurs,
prepared way for man.

Patterns

How did the tree know
way to drop its leaves to form
patterns on the ground?

Rows

Harvest Moon on high.
Rows of cornshocks in the fields.
Frost covers the ground.

Tug

"Rest in peace," the preacher said.
Then battle started.
It's who gets what and how much.

Kaleidoscope

Autumn leaves all falling down.
Covering the ground.
It's nature's kaleidoscope.

Migration

The sun was cooling,
and the planets cooled also.
Martians moved to earth.

Meal

Golden, flowing wheat.
Good for many things we eat.
Locust swarm ate all.

Moving

Sun cooling, Martians moved to earth.
Sun is still cooling
Next move: Earthlings to Venus.

Up

Old Faithful geyser
spurts up water every hour.
It's nature's hiccup.

Voyage

If you want to leave this world,
but want to come back.
Sit down at your computer.

Question

So, what is nature?
Don't ask me, only God knows.
He made it all.

Song

Nature abhors a vacuum;
That's when fools rush in.
Oops! Can't forget that love song.

Leaving

Sun was in heating cycle.
Earth too hot for life.
Pack all for journey to Mars.

Balk

Last man in jump string.
Chicken; didn't jump. Later, learned
all of string were killed.

Thread

The spinning wheel is magic.
It makes thread from gold.
But can it make gold from thread?

Surprise

While wandering through the Louvre,
I saw a strange sight.
Sculpture: man standing on head.

Peak

Matterhorn is famous.
And so are they who climb it.
Is that why it's there?

Scholar

"Went to Harvard and Yale,"
he boasted. "And you?"
I went to school of hard knocks.

Grammar

It was thee and thou and ye.
That was yesteryear.
Today, pal, it's me and youse.

Loose

Society's looser now.
And from the look of things
the brain is also.

Expectation

The quiet serenity
of the mountain peak
was shattered by avalanche.

Sign

Long days at sea; where was land?
Compass broke. Cloudy.
A lone Albatross flew by.

Help

I need some inspiration.
Got any to spare?
Couldn't find it anywhere.

It's yours

Go get on the Internet.
Make bet; buy a pet.
It's all there for the asking.

Where is It

It's the age of miracles.
Man-made, that is.
Until you really want one.

Got It All

Imagination takes you anywhere,
anytime, anything.
What you see is what you get.

Who's Who

I approached the computer,
Said, "I'm the Master."
Turned on, screen read, "I'm Master."

Crossing

We met at railroad crossing.
You and your girlfriend?
No. Was my car and the train.

Limit

My car has dozens of dents
from friendly drivers.
Got ticket, over dent limit.

Lunch

We both reached for our wallets
to pay for lunch check.
Somehow, mine stuck in pocket.

Goodbye

Old homestead is on the block.
Lived there many years.
I let it go, shed some tears.

Forget It

Your memories can haunt you.
Things done right and wrong.
Lucky amnesiacs.

Stump

He's out stumping now.
You mean he's running for office?
No, cutting down trees.

Answers

How many people must die
Before we all see
War is never the answer?

Reward

Platoon totally wiped out.
General ordered
Posthumous Medals to all.

Fearsome

In field, a fearsome scarecrow
with his arms outstretched.
On one arm, a fearless crow.

Pals

Scarecrow called friend in next field.
"Seen any crows, pal?"
Crow answered, "No! "Not today."

Party

Scarecrow in a field of corn
got very lonely.
Invited crows to join him.

Where

The bugle sounded retreat.
All men turned and ran.
Shot in back instead of front.

Good

What makes good soldier?
Training, skill, bravery too,
Plus a lot of luck,

Message

Sent message to my brother.
Was a cannon ball.
He received it; no answer.

Carnage

The sight, sound and smell
of the dead and the dying
sicken those living.

Long Way

"It's a long way to Tipperary,"
sang boys in trenches.
Many never made it there.

Fly

Protected from winter cold,
inside our warm house,
lives our resident housefly.

Past

All that was "is," is past.
There is no more "is," these days.
Future, present are gone.

Survive

What does love need to survive?
It doesn't need much.
All it really needs is love.

Failure

It's a flaw in man
that, when the heart takes over,
the brain will shut down.

Know

Can you be in love
and not know it? Yes, you can;
but you will show it.

Wounds

Love's wounds are invisible.
But yes, they are there.
And these wounds are so pleasant.

Awakening

Why did she have to die,
for me to realize
how much I really loved her?

Lost

Her lips were like rose petals.
Kissed her once, again.
Mind went blank, heart took over.

All

Thought I gave you all my love.
But still have much more.
Sad you can no more receive.

Life

Did you have to die
for me to understand life?
Its bliss and strife.

Act

A shot rang out.
A body thumped to the floor.
Curtain closed, act one.

Sad

Grandchildren have gone.
House is very quiet now.
Lone tear on her cheek.

Help

Pen, paper ready.
Waiting for inspiration.
The telephone rang.

Diva

The Diva sang her heart out.
Is she all right now?
Yes, she received a transplant.

Flight

Stewardess asked me,
"Have you flown much before?"
"No! My arms get tired."

Load

Ant had heavy load.
Asked him if he wanted help.
"No. Thanks, bud," he said.

Transition

The red setting sun.
Another day now is done.
Now night has begun.

Turns

Day creatures about.
Dark brings end of that, but now.
Night creatures have turn.

Whodunit

"Who done it?" asked detective.
They said, ask butler.
Try again, on vacation.

Misquote

Give me liberty
or nothing else. Slight difference
from Patrick Henry

Hanging

My only regret
is that you're hanging me.
Was that Nathan Hale?

Merciful

Fine piano wire
will make a very good noose.
Don't last long with that.

Trip

"Mommy, can I go to the moon?"
Busy Mom answered,
"Go ask your Father dear."

Fortune

Finished Astrology cards.
Three hundred sixty-five.
Shuffled them, put on dates and signs.

Haiku Moment

On my way to town
I had a Haiku moment.
Way home forgot it.

Full Shine

Two lovers on a bright night,
doing what they do
by the light of a full earth.

Sequence

Night follows the day.
It's an endless cycle. Or
does day follow night?

Cares

"Oh! Who cares?" I lamented.
Wasn't really fair.
Someone cared for fifty years.

End

Does time have an end?
Will we ever know?
Is it when, where, why, how?

Fall

Leaves falling to ground.
Autumn, winter close behind.
Geese flock flying south.

Hands

We walked down the path
holding hands, hearts beating fast.
Path's end, we parted.

School

School bells rang loudly.
But the classrooms were empty.
It was Saturday.

Spring

'Twas first breath of spring.
And winter's last dying gasp.
Crocus peeked through snow.

Hills

I live on a hill
and so does everyone else
in this mountain state.

Winds

Autumn winds blow leaves,
falling from trees, scuttling on ground.
Squirrel scurries by.

Pressure

Waiting in the doctor's office,
my blood pressure soared
as cute nurse was going by

Nature

Cut down trees, pave over grass.
Can't we do better?
Must we always destroy nature?

Strange

Lunar observatory
sighted strange creatures.
They look odd, those earth people.

Eclipse

Eclipse of sun, dark.
Never became light again.
Moon refused to budge.

Unknown

No one knew who we were then.
No one knows it now,
And no one will ever know.

What

'Twas an exciting story.
Was it fact or fiction?
Do you really want to know?

Dark Side

Passing by dark side of moon,
we saw many lights.
Unknown civilization.

Desire

Lunar mountain top.
Looked up at the shining earth
Must go there sometime.

Nobody

Most of my childhood friends gone.
Nobody knew me.
Not my home town anymore.

Night

Stars shining brightly.
The night was dark and quiet.
Large meteor struck.

Life

Birds fly and fish swim.
Mammals walk on the earth.
Life takes many forms.

Nature

Nature's wonders can't be told.
They are young and old.
They are as precious as gold.

Writing

Writing Haiku can be fun
Puts mind on the run
Covers all under the sun.

Trip

The rocket-ship to the moon
will be leaving soon.
All aboard for Honeymoon.

Peaceful

Waving fields of wheat.
Sun shining brightly above.
A meadowlark sings.

Calm

Clear blue sky above.
Puffy white clouds floating by.
Hawk circles idly.

All Aboard

Engine snorted steam, coughed smoke,
lumbered from station,
then sped gracefully down tracks.

Man

Sun shines, moon shines, stars twinkle.
Universe moves on
With bumbling Man in its wake.

Difference

Are women different from men?
We often ask that.
But none cares or dares answer.

Climb

"Mountain climbing?" asked a friend.
"Must check better half."
"You mean your wife?" "No my legs."

Tree

Small child's first Yule Tree.
She looked in wide eyed wonder.
Ran to hug, both fell.

Answer

Stood on a high mountain top.
Shouted, "Why're we here?"
Answer came back, "Why're we here?"

Tornado

Tornado picked up my car.
Dropped us in next town.
Ticket: "Illegally parked."

Necessary

Your mind is a complex thing.
Makes you laugh, cry, sing.
Without it, no human being.

Flowers

Golden sun above.
Field full of wild flowers.
Humming bird hovers.

Aunt

My aunt lived in the country.
Coal stove, water pump.
She still baked best apple pie.

Nickel

Dad, how was Great Depression?
Tough, nickel bought all.
Oh, that sounds like fun.

Branded

Sun time is fun time.
Lying on sand, getting brand.
White on breast, rear and tummy.

Orbit

First orbit of the moon
was made by my Jersey cow.
She jumped over it.

Been

"Where are you going?"
"Nowhere," the wise guy quipped.
"I've been there, done that."

Trip

"Going to the moon."
"Don't forget raincoat and rubbers,"
my Mom reminded.

Expendable

Attack was successful.
There was only one man killed
But he was my son.

Place

Dead and dying have no place
in the human race.
It's only for the living.

Where

Stars twinkled, soft music played.
We danced night away.
I never saw her again.

Voyager

Bathroom busy all the time.
At end of voyage,
stranger walked off ship

Time

I'm in a time warp.
It's twenty-first century.
I'm in twentieth.

Transplant

I need life transplant.
My life now is not working.
Have to find donor.

Fish

Dropped line in water.
Fish swam up, flipped tail and left.
He'd been there, done that.

Cycles

Life goes in cycles.
There are ups and there are downs.
When up, get prepared.

Score

Quarterback threw ball.
It landed in goal post net.
Now, what is the score?

Seas

Stormy seas were high;
washed over rails of ship.
A fish flopped on deck.

Meadow

Running through meadow.
High grass thrashing round my legs.
Scared grasshopper leaped.

Wrong Side

Got up on wrong side of bed.
Was it a bad day?
No, it was still dark outside.

Moon

I gazed at the moon on high.
While wondering why.
Was it there for you and I?

Aqua

What is H_2O?
A gas, liquid or solid?
Nature's mysteries.

Bang

Started with big bang.
Man developed over time.
Ended with big bang.

Glacier

Ice age creeps down from the north.
Water hits new low.
Showing lands ne'er seen before.

Full Moon

Is that full moon up above
for me and my love,
or just an earth satellite?

Sounds

How he longed to hear
animal sounds of nature.
They're all extinct now.

Grass

National Paving Project,
well underway.
Must leave space for grass acre.

Train

Waiting for the train one day
on station platform.
Express went thundering by.

Load

Air Force pilot dropped his load.
Couldn't help thinking,
"How many won't wake tomorrow?"

Stare

Enemy soldier's blank stare.
Oozing wound in chest.
Wiped blood off my bayonet.

Hot

It's that time again.
Sun starting to heat up.
Time to leave for Mars.

Cold

Ice age came with a vengeance.
Earth one big ice cube.
Pack and move to Venus.

Tide

The sun tide ebbs and flows
every billion years.
We move from Earth, Venus, Mars.

Stair

You were standing on the stair.
I could only stare.
First time I saw an Angel.

Union

Universes collided.
Now, two suns; two earths.
Met some ancient relatives.

Traveler

I am a traveling salesman.
Universe, my beat.
Mercury, Earth, Pluto, all.

Mover

Getting around Universe
is much easier now.
Shuttle bus back in operation.

Christmas

Christmas Eve in no man's land.
Both sides stopped shooting.
Met, sang carols together

Pat

Sometimes when sitting, thinking,
in despair sinking,
Guardian Angel pats shoulder.

Christmas Eve Sounds

Heard footsteps on my roof.
Was it Santa's deer?
No, a couple of fat crows.

Carols

Please don't sing Carols!
I've got no one to sing with;
Not home for Christmas

Cure

Love will find a way
to heal all those heartfelt wounds.
Just give it a chance.

Solution

Late night, pondering.
Problems, problems; wondering.
Solved! I fell asleep.

Citizen

Citizen of this or that.
We're all human beings.
Why can't we live together?

Wonder

"I just want to be happy,"
she said many times.
Don't know if she ever was.

Chance

'Twas a chance romance.
But must have been more than that
to last fifty years.

Turn

Loaded gun with five shells.
My friend took first shot.
No fire, handed it to me.

Thankless

Took everything for granted.
Not appreciated.
Now have lots of time to think.

Roulette

Spun the cylinder.
Put gun to head, pulled trigger.
Handed to next man.

Game

First man started game.
One shell, spin, pull the trigger.
Maybe next man's turn.

Power

If you are really in love.
You'll take on the world.
Nothing is too difficult.

Win

Were you ever a winner
and you didn't know?
You probably are one now.

Hope

It's just a card game.
So what if you lost the ranch?
Try again tomorrow.

Why

Tell me, why is happiness
such an elusive thing?
If I knew, I'd be happy.

Bell

When that bell begins to toll,
will it be for you?
If so, you will not hear it.

Life

The world will continue on
long after I'm gone.
Did my life make a difference?

Count

Call it what you want.
Long green, lettuce, moolah, cash.
If you ain't got, tough.

Priority

Pave over that grass,
and cut down all those big trees.
We're building condos.

Think

I write between tears,
thinking of all those years;
both sadness and cheers.

Mess

Park Street is a mess,
but so is the whole damn town.
Does anyone care?

Force

Forget about love.
It's the money, stupid,
makes the world go 'round.

Decision

Most of the trees gone.
So is oxygen.
Do we need to plant more trees?

Away

You're far away now.
Farther than ever before.
How can I reach you?

Girl

The girl of your dreams!
When you finally meet her
you'll be wide awake.

Cloud

On a cloud up in the sky,
there'll be you and I
free from pain and sorrow.

Sunrise

Sunrise, all is bright.
Gone all those fears of the night.
Life can be delight.

Dementia

Lived in third dimension, bored.
Tried two dimensions, flat.
Will now try fourth dimension.

Star

Looking at you, star;
Wondering if there you are.
Or are you now dead.

Morn

Misty morning sky.
Dew-covered fields and trees.
Sun ray peeked o’er hills.

Response

Disaster, what now.
First call in all reporters.
And then write a book.

Fixit

Universal light dimmed out.
Sent rapid repair
Up and running, good as new

Separation

Bad earthquake; 7.5.
Standing on back porch.
Garage twenty miles away.

Disaster

It's a disaster!
Earthquake, twister, typhoon, what?
No, it's my hairdo.

Glory

Heroes all of them;
some alive and some now dead.
Was it all worth it?

Over

Over top, ‘cross no man’s land.
Some make it, some don’t.
Some will come back and some won’t.

Hunter

A bounty hunter hunts bounty.
So what is bounty?
We’ll know that when he finds it.

Rockets

Rockets’ red glare through the day
and all through the night.
Flag still there by morning’s light.

Wrong

Shell came in; it was a dud.
Name on it was Joe.
Joe gone, it was not his turn.

Chaos

My life's in chaos;
I've got to get organized.
Oh well, maybe tomorrow.

Arrival

Blossoms in the spring.
Ground mushy from melting snow.
First robin arrives.

See-Saw

Sat down on the see-saw.
My friend jumped off other end.
Hit ground with a thump.

Round

The merry-go-round
goes round and round. Grab brass ring;
get another ride.

Summer

Summer time is lazy time.
Lying in the sun;
soaking up those golden rays.

Old Days

Ah! Those good old days.
Outhouse, water pump, coal stove.
Was that really good?

Soaring

Soaring 'mongst the clouds!
Only sound was whispering wind.
Ground coming up fast.

Bum

I got a bum steer.
You mean some bad advice?
No, ‘twas lazy bull.

Bags

Quartermaster said,
“Order lots of body bags.
This one will be tough.”

Glory

He was covered with glory.
You mean those medals?
No, I mean morning glory.

Christmas

Finished wrapping Christmas gifts.
Forgot to mark them.
Get busy, unwrap, rewrap.

Santa

Santa came down the chimney.
Saw all the presents.
"Good job Pop! Check back next year."

Style

Style is what we are told.
It can be new or old.
It's what's in stores to be sold.

Wonder

At some future time,
will someone dig up my bones,
wonder who I was?

Fate

Tragedy strikes all.
Whether you are big or small.
You just keep living.

Phones

Only a phone call away.
That what cell phones say.
So grab your phone and let's talk.

Thoughts

My mind is a blank.
That's the way it's always been
and always will be.

Sharp

"He's sharp as a tack."
They said about the old man.
But what's a tack know?

Traveling

All my boyhood dreams came true.
Traveled round the world.
And on the way I met you.

Never

Will there ever be?
Another one like she?
No, not for me.

Remember

When tragedy strikes,
just build a memorial.
That makes it alright.

Anyone

Dead and dying everywhere.
Does anyone care?
Not the ones who sent them there.

Remembering

The high profile dead
will get a memorial.
But not the commoners.

Statue

Big statue in park.
Who was that guy anyway?
No one remembers.

Fame

He's a famous man.
What did he do that's so great?
Well, he talked a lot.

Politico

Politician came to town
Gave a speech in park;
Lots of talk, didn't say much.

Life

Heard life can be beautiful.
Sitting here alone,
know it can be miserable.

Colors

Bright colored walls and sunsets.
That's the Grand Canyon.
It's nature's kaleidoscope.

Nature

Nature can be kind or cruel.
Sunlight and showers.
Typhoons, tornadoes, earthquakes.

Songs

I think old songs are the best.
But not when too old.
Then they are my Mother's songs.

Blue

Am I ever blue?
The answer to that is "Yes.
When I think of you."

Lost

Always wondered what I'd do
if I should lose you.
I still don't know the answer.

Sitting

Sitting, what to do?
Looked out window, was raining.
Went back to sitting.

Eyes

Oriental eyes.
They look up into the skies.
Thinking of gone byes.

Winner

I took chance on love.
The payoff was really great.
Lasted for fifty years.

Way to Go

The thruway was jammed.
Bumper to bumper traffic.
Motorbike zipped by.

Relax

I let my eyes close.
And I let my mind roam free.
Saw many new things.

Life

Where did my life go astray?
Never did I say
I wanted what is today.

The End

Standing before firing squad
to be shot as spy.
In cold sweat when I woke up.

Life

Was my whole life just a dream?
Was it really true?
Or was it a book I read?

There

Were you really there?
Or was it just a movie?
Sometimes I wonder.

Scene

In those big brown eyes,
Saw a life of constant bliss.
Sealed it with a kiss.

Survival

Life's complicated.
You are in over your head;
time to start swimming.

NYC

Life in New York City.
Is that really a living,
or just existence?

Dice

When the dice were rolled,
shattered in many pieces;
formed the Universe.

Sides

Man is like the moon.
He has both dark and light sides.
Which one do we see?

Inspiration

Pass out more medals.
We need to inspire these men
to die for country.

Strange

‘Twas a strange romance.
They gazed up at the full moon.
T-rex and Diplod.

Mixed

Parents did not approve it.
‘Twas a mixed marriage.
Cro-Magnon, Neanderthal.

Enemies

On paper we were enemies.
We were taught to hate.
But if you love, you can’t hate.

Eternal

Sunlight, moonlight, eternal.
Seen for millions years
by dinosaurs and, now, man.

Thanks

Not much at saying thank you,
even when I care.
But the feeling is there.

Position

They told me it was gridlock.
You mean traffic jam?
No, firing coordinates.

Talk

Lecturer finished his speech.
Asked for questions.
No response, all were dozing.

Truth

World's a lousy mess.
Leaders lying through their teeth.
It's all about greed.

Fighting

Generals want war.
Privates do all the fighting.
Generals get credit.

War

War kills enemies, friends.
Those who die can't complain.
The living don't seem to care.

Odds

The sun was happy and smiled.
Then angry Thor roared.
But happy sun just smiled back.

Life

Can you put back the pieces
of a broken life?
Yes, if you try really hard.

Future

I looked deep into her eyes.
And, to my surprise,
saw what my life would comprise.

Say What

It's easy to say
life is good when it is good;
when it's not, it's not.

Meddler

Man is the only creature
who makes what's simple
into what's complicated.

Own

I'm my own worst enemy.
There's nobody else
who treats me the way I do.

Buck

Clouds drift through the sky.
Winds whisper a lullaby.
A proud buck bounds by.

Closed

Closed eyes to shut out world.
Just temporary.
Opened eyes, world was still there.

Knew

First time I kissed her,
lips as soft as rose petals.
Knew I was in love.

Gift

He gave us all life.
Should be appreciated.
It’s not ours to take.

How

Slice tomatoes, bread.
Butter bread, add tomatoes.
Make tomato sandwich.

Interaction

The chemistry was not there.
Was that really bad?
No, there was ‘lectricity.

Duty

Uncle said we have to fight;
We are in the right.
So then we fought and we won.

Story

Every life has a story.
We want to survive.
Some do it well, some do not.

Bad

Greed and corruption
can cause an eruption
called revolution.

Faults

Human beings are not perfect;
they have many faults.
We must tolerate those faults.

Meaning

I was on a roll.
You mean a streak of good luck?
No, I'm a hot dog.

Do It

Sharks lived for millions of years.
Time cannot kill them.
But man will do what time can't.

Old Timer

“How old are you?” I asked croc.
“I’m millions of years.
And you, Homo Sapiens?”

Rainbow

Went to the end of rainbow;
looked for pot of gold.
No gold, but I did find you.

Bell

Bong, bong, the bell tolled.
Was the bell tolling for me?
Can’t be, I heard it.

Returned

Thousands were sent off to war.
Many, no return
Dads, moms, sisters, brothers grieved.

Power

Stronger than the wind,
the sun, tide and gravity,
is the power of love .

Who

Pyramids are grand.
Towering high above the sand.
Were they made by man?

Late

Peace came a little too late
for one lone soldier.
Killed just before armistice.

Final

Graves' registration soldier
removed man's dog tag.
Then zipped open a body bag.

Companion

Held hands in movie.
Shared a soda afterward.
Then we shared a life.

Guide

Space is dark and deep
but you will not lose your way.
The stars will guide you.

Change

What man starts thin then gets fat?
Then gets thin again?
It is the man in the moon.

Winner

When you have a winning hand,
there's no losing.
You can bet the ranch on it.

Red

"Mars is a dead planet,"
say astronomers.
But not natives who live there.

Truth

Did I ever tell the truth?
Yes, about one thing
'T was when I said I love you.

Life

Elusive as thought
is tranquility in life.
You'll seek it in vain.

Round

Life's Merry Go Round goes round
faster and faster.
You're not able to get off.

Work

Yes, working for a living
can be a chore.
But no work can be a bore.

Lifetime

So, how long is a lifetime?
It is 'eternal'?
There's really no end to life?

Blessed

So, blessed are those people
who ask for naught.
They're happy with what they've got.

Royal

If I were a Prince,
she would have been my Princess.
She was anyway.

Maybe

Did all that really happen?
Was it just a dream?
Sometimes I can't help wondering.

Different

Some have betrayed their country,
but this is different;
my country has betrayed me.

Served

Forefathers wrote it.
It has served our country well.
Now we've torn it up.

Forms

Despots come in many forms.
So does the devil.
Hard to see the difference.

Angel

Can an Angel be human?
I believe they can,
because I knew one who was.

Know

"What is love?" you ask.
When it does happen to you,
you won't have to ask.

Concerned

Heard the siren sound.
It meant much to those concerned,
but no one else cared.

Question

I heard a voice one morning.
It asked a question.
Will you destroy everything.

Decisions

We make decisions.
Some are right and some are wrong.
/ Nobody's perfect.

Rain Drops

Bombs were falling like rain drops.
Dead lay in the streets.
Why do they do this to us.

Inside

I lived in myself for years.
Then tragedy struck.
Had to come out in the world.

Talk

Politicians talk.
But do they say anything?
That is the question.

Comparison

Infinity and eternity
are the ultimate.
Man is so small in all this.

Part

In our marriage vows we said,
"Till death do us part."
And that's the way it happened.

Life

I'm going through the motions,
trying to pretend
this is really still a life.

Story

What is fiction? What is fact?
Often cannot tell.
Sit back; enjoy the story.

No Problem

"Don't worry 'bout casualties;
can get more soldiers,"
was the general's order.

Believe

You will be in big trouble
if ever you should
believe your publicity.

Thief

The "Thief of Baghdad"
was a great motion picture.
But now it's the truth.

Farm

It was baa, oink, moo and neigh.
Pleasant barnyard sounds.
Battlefield crying, moaning.

Back

Uncle wanted him.
It was only for one year.
He never came back.

Different

Loneliness down here
is no different from up there.
It's still loneliness.

Long

Man's path is endless.
Genesis, eternity.
Game for the journey?

Nothing New

Crusaders crushed the Moslems.
Thousand years later.
We are doing it again.

Other

That other world.
Where is it and who is there?
Who knows the answer?

Around

Wheel of life goes round.
What was once will be again,
but where does it stop?

Sad

When you're feeling blue,
and you don't know what to do,
then whistle a tune.

Fame

Generals famous –
they're in the history books.
Not Privates; they're dead.

Game

To generals, war's a game.
To privates, not the same.
Generals plot; privates die.

Law

Killing is against the law.
Divine and manmade.
So how does war make it right?

Shake

The earth shakes, rattles and rolls.
It's called an earthquake.
It will never be a hit.

Thought

I was cerebrating.
That's "deep thought" to you.
It can give you a headache.

When

I always wondered,
"When will I ever grow up?"
I'm still wondering.

Child

Perpetual child.
So full of fun and mischief.
He never grew up.

Odd Ones

Creatures far beneath the sea.
They are enduring.
Here longer then you and me.

Moving

The earth never sleeps.
It is in constant motion.
Inside and outside.

Spell

How do you spell "war?"
Not "W A R;"
It's "D E A T H."

Fight

It was raining cats and dogs.
They fought furiously.
You know dogs never liked cats.

Snowy Peak

The snow-capped mountain
was sleeping for many years.
Woke up with a bang.

Shower

Caught in a summer shower.
Miserable and drenched.
Until we saw the rainbow.

Big Boy

I marveled at Mount Everest.
Mother nature said,
"He is just a growing boy."

Peace

So they finally made peace.
Religions, races?
Not that, it was cats and dogs.

Truce

Finally called a truce.
Christians, Jews, Moslems, white, black?
No, it was the dogs and cats.

Home

The Senior Center
was my home away from home.
I really miss it.

Friends

All the friends I made
will never be forgotten.
Engraved in my mind.

Ordinary

Nothing special about him.
Mediocre man;
except to his family.

Catch

A rainbow is beautiful,
but you can't catch it.
It's really an illusion.

Pot

That old pot of gold
is not at end of rainbow.
It's the whole rainbow.

Needle

Somewhere in that pile of straw
there is a needle.
Forget it, buy a new one.

Future

He gave no thought to the future.
So it gave no thought to him.
That's why we'll never know him.

Remember

We made the world of today,
whether good or bad.
Now they want to forget us.

Winter

A dead leaf blowing
over the windswept snow-scape.
A squirrel scampers by.

Mind

Your mind has infinite power.
It can compress time.
Brings back long past happenings.

Right

For my country, I fight.
They tell me it's right.
So, 'Thou shalt not kill,' forget.

Fought

He fought for his country.
He also died for his country.
Who remembers that?

Contact

We merely touched hands.
Two hearts beat out in Morse code.
They said, "I love you."

Feeling

Joy is a feeling you have.
So is sorrow.
You can make it what you want.

Progress

Human discourse is extinct;
now talk to computers.
What will be man's next advance?

Too Late

Regrets and remorse.
I ask, "Why did I do that?"
or "Why didn't I?"

Remains

Just their names on stone.
That's all there is left of them.
Were they really here?

Big Shots

People at the top,
who make the big decisions,
often not too smart.

Why

First we destroy things.
Then we build them up again.
But does this make sense?

Wet or Dry

I jumped into the swimming pool.
Kersplash, water flew.
Everyone got wet but me.

Go

Something, somewhere told me,
Go to Germany.
Someone there needs you.

Time

All my friends were gone.
I felt bad but then I heard,
Wait, it's not your time.

Saving

Can your life work be
to save one single person?
I think so, I did.

Missing

My life has been a circle.
South, North, South again.
But now something is missing.

No One

If you have no family,
and also no friends,
life can be really lonely.

Name

What's the meaning of lonely?
Call it what you want,
it's not a pleasant feeling.

Journey

All life is a one way trip.
It's always forward;
everyone to the same end.

Ape

Monkeys watch humans,
do exactly what we do.
Don't monkey with monkeys.

Change

I left my old home
and now I have made new friends.
Somehow not the same.

Going

Smiling through the tears,
pretending there were no fears,
I said goodbye to all.

Names

Just their names on stone,
That's all there is left of them.
Were they really here?

Snow

Biggest snowstorm of the year;
footprints quickly filled,
left no trace of man or beast.

Never

In the game of life,
you never know when break comes,
so never give up.

Man One

Man is no different
no matter where he may live.
Good, bad everywhere.

Man Two

The intelligence of man
is universal.
It knows no worldly bounds.

Man Three

So, will man survive
his own nefarious deeds?
Only time will tell.

Civil

Brother fought brother.
They both shot and they both bled.
They died embracing.

Life

The trouble with life
is that you are so busy,
no time to live it.

The End

Man has capability
to destroy himself.
What will he do about it?

Unlikely

A big city girl
met a naïve small town boy.
Became lifelong match.

Different

They laugh, they cry and they bleed
the same way we do.
Why are they the enemy?

Sign

Alien ship landed at galactaport.
They saw sign reading,
"Sorry, no greens allowed here."

Where

Sitting in the coffee shop,
people going by.
All hurrying nowhere.

Waves

The waves roll in on the beach.
They're never ending,
under sun or under moon.

Cost

I was in my ship to Mars.
Control panel flashed;
put in another quarter.

Answer

"So, why are we here?"
a small voice was heard to ask.
There was no answer.

All Gone

Lived in desert; teeming life.
Moved to big city;
It was a real wasteland.

Companion

'Twas a lonely trip,
Just me and man in the moon.
He stayed all the way.

Away

Millions of stars shone brightly;
so did a full moon.
The bombardier dropped his load.

Master

Fate's a cruel master.
You've no control over it;
may be good or bad.

Open

They tried to unlock
all the mystery of life.
Op'ed Pandora's box.

Lesson

Can man learn from the past?
Judging from present,
the answer to that is no.

Why

Everything is gone.
All the things I knew in life.
Why I am still here.

Powerless

All life is a mystery:
birth, living and death;
for we are not in control.

Passing

Like sand in an hourglass
time goes quietly by.
We can do naught to stop it.

Fill

You will get voids in your life
which you cannot fill.
Don't try, just go on living.

Lost

It happened in a flash.
I was completely conquered
by two charming eyes.

Shed

It was not his blood they shed.
'Twas that of others.
Didn't hurt him a bit.

Past

Why do I live in the past?
The past is past.
Why not leave it all alone?

Away

There is nothing more lonely
than a young soldier
who is far away from home

Hue

White, black, yellow, red.
So why can't someone be green?
Think about that one.

Paths

Beware of the easy path.
It may appear easier;
may have many hidden traps.

Life

My life was like the clouds.
Constantly changing.
Sometimes here and sometimes not.

Puffy

Puffy masses overhead.
Look like this, then that.
Never the same again.

Why

My life has ended,
but I am still present.
Can you explain that?

Horses

Wild horse hooves pounded earth.
Till enslaved by man,
they were free as you and I.

Bagged

He pulled the trigger.
Saw him slump to earth.
Beautiful twelve point.

Clouds

Drifting clouds up in the sky.
Now you're here; then not.
Where do you go when you're gone?

How Long

Sparkling waterfall.
Will you flow eternally,
or just a billion years?

Moon

Listening to song, “Blue Moon.”
Don’t see any blue.
Was composer color blind?

Words

Which one is greater
infinity, eternity?
Words without meaning.

Win

If you want to play by rules,
you won’t always win.
Sometimes need to break the rules.

Help

If you count on luck,
you may get into trouble.
Better stack the deck.

Romance

Like two ships that pass in the night.
No, it was different;
like two big rigs colliding.

View

Winner called it good luck.
Loser said cheating.
It's all in your point of view.

All

Lost whole family in war.
Hit by a dumb bomb.
We're all resting in peace now.

Boats

All our earthly boats
float on a sea of lava,
on endless journeys.

Venus

The Venusian was chilly
so he took a dip
in volcano's warm lava.

Decision

They say, "Go with the flow,"
but what do they know?
Sometimes have to swim upstream.

Reward

For the general,
A large statue on a horse.
For private, small cross.

Forgotten

I think the world forgot me.
But what do I care.
I forgot it long ago.

Prayer

Each morning we kneel and pray.
We kill more that day.
Why? They are the enemy.

Journey

We're in the same boat,
Drifting through the universe.
Let's not rock the boat.

Power

He found ultimate power;
decided to use it.
Now he's gone, and so is earth.

Thinking

Philosophy is talk, talk,
with no solutions
and also no conclusions.

Lies

The government lies to us,
and so does the press.
Where can we find out the truth?

Journey

Traveled thousands of miles
over land and sea.
Seed took root in Kansas field.

Change

What is right and what is wrong?
Changes day to day.
My conscience is getting tired.

Might

One person said, “Might makes right.”
But we disagreed.
Now it seems that it is true.

Life

Gladness, sadness, I've seen it all.
I've been up and down.
Now all I want is peace.

The End

Death, why did you come here?
I didn't call you.
Why couldn't you have waited?

Church

A church is a place
in which you can rest your soul.
Make body and mind whole.

Poor

Poverty is everywhere.
Why couldn't we share?
Some have so much they could spare.

Meaning

What is the meaning of life?
I had no answer.
Asked others, still no answer.

Ordinary

Just an ordinary guy,
nothing ever great.
But never hurt anyone.

Thoughts

Haunted by so many thoughts,
some good and some bad.
How can we erase all that?

Memories

Yet so many memories.
Good, bad, happy, sad.
Remember good, forget bad.

Answer

We do not know the answer.
They say wise men do.
If so, why don't they tell us?

Down and out

Nothing matters anymore.
Life has come and gone.
It's not the same anymore.

Lost

While hunting for that needle,
I moved a lot of straw.
Must have lost it somewhere else

Peace

Peace, you fleeting thing.
We want you so bad
that we fight wars to get you.

Only One

The Sergeant told us,
it takes only one bullet
if in the right place.

Obscured

Sights, sounds of nature
are obliterated by
men and their machines.

Which

What's cruel and inhuman act:
Beating a prisoner
or bombing civilians?

Message

One day a robin
came to me with a message.
It said, "Spring is here."

Too Late

"Heh! Put out those lights!"
Air Raid Warden hollered,
just before bomb struck.

Luck

Sitting on a cloud he said,
"Was lucky in last war;
will I be so in this one?"

Free

All serfs and slaves have been freed.
That's what we are told.
Looking around, I wonder.

Spirit

Listening to Rachmaninoff,
master of the keys,
spirit traveled far and wide.

Change

Everything is going wrong.
We must do something.
We need to reorganize.

When

I live in the past.
The present is too painful,
future uncertain.

What

When you reach the great beyond,
life on earth is done.
Then what will be there for you?

Conquest

He conquered infinite space;
found eternal life.
He was never seen again.

Time

There was no future.
There was no present or past.
Time had stopped ticking.

Life

Past, present, future.
Is that all there is to life?
Must be something more.

Continue

Aching body, fevered brain.
But life must go on.
No one knows the reason why.

Hero

Grimy, hungry and homeless.
Walked into pawn shop.
Sold his medal of honor.

Heroes

Both of them received medals.
One, pinned on his chest.
The other, laid on his stone.

Eternal

Though volcanoes roar
and earthquakes also rumble,
man will still go on.

Over

Regrets and remorse.
If that is all that is left,
time to close the game.

Order

A flood of thoughts came tumbling.
My mind was fumbling
to make order of chaos.

Know

So ignorant is the man
who thinks he knows all;
and he'll never learn.

Expert

He was an expert.
Knew the name of every star,
whether live or dead.

Books

Standing in the library,
got a dreadful thought.
I'll never read all these books.

Sawing

He sawed most vigorously
on a wooden box.
Oh! He's first violinist!

Company

Sitting 'mongst a crowd
of laughing, talking people.
I was all alone.

Tired

I was bone tired and weary.
Aren't these the same thing?
Anyway, that's how tired I was.

Justice

They say justice is blind.
From some decisions,
we have to believe that's true.

Finally

"What was that flash in the sky?"
Martian boy asked mother.
"I think the earth exploded."

Where

"So where did it go?"
asked returning Astronaut.
"'Twas here when I left."

Careful

I reached for a star.
I only got my hand burnt.
So don't reach too far.

Know

We live and we die.
But does anyone know why?
Or that we passed by?

Catch

Joy flees before us
no matter how we pursue;
always out of reach.

Huh

What is the new craze?
It changes from year to year;
hard to keep up with.

Confined

They're no more debtors' prisons.
Now they've been replaced
with political prisons.

Moolah

Congress moves money around
like a croupier
in a Vegas Casino.

Like Us

Kings are made not born.
They're blood is red like ours.
Blueblood is a myth.

Advantage

Man exploits all earth's creatures.
But that's not the worst.
He exploits his fellow man.

Forsooth

"No," my fortune teller said
"It's not in the cards."
I told her, "Try a new deck."

Life

You have to live life.
It's just like riding a bike.
Have to keep moving.

Eyes

When I cry, tears sting my eyes.
But that's not as bad
as the pain that's in my heart.

Pep Talk

Coach said, "Butt heads, use elbows.
This is no tea party.
Want to see lots of bruises!"

Practical

I've been a practical man.
Measurements, machines.
Never knew philosophy.

Remembrance

So we sent them off to die.
But we'll make it right.
Just build a nice monument.

Help

He was repeat offender.
Raised in poverty.
Was only trying to live.

Alert

Their muscles tired and aching,
they move ‘bout slowly.
But their minds are sharp and clear.

Maybe

We made a new world,
but is it a better world?
Only time will tell.

Careful

“Hoopster, how high can you jump?”
He crouched and leapt.
So high, broke a leg landing.

88

Was great on eighty-eight.
You mean piano?
No, it was German cannon.

Destiny

Nations rise and fall.
Their star burns brightly then fades.
None can escape this.

Gatherings

Family dinners on Sundays.
Kids, grandkids and wife.
All gone now; I'm all alone.

Last

'Twas the last day in my old house.
All those empty rooms.
Gave me an empty feeling

Home

Empty house and empty heart.
Lived there many years.
Leaving brings a few tears.

Present

We have the future and the past.
Present never lasts.
It’s either coming or gone.

Today

Tomorrow is eternal,
as is yesterday.
Today is never-lasting.

Wait

Will we wait another fifty years?
Another ocean of tears.
Till we honor them again.

Know

You know you’re alone.
when you want to say something
and no one is there.

Gone

Rubble piled in the streets
as high as the second floor.
Wurzburg was no more.

Ring

I miss the church bells
that rang on Sunday morning.
Such a peaceful sound.

Shine

The sun shines on all of us,
wherever we are.
So be happy in your life.

Us

Some are famous, some are not.
Some are rich, some poor.
But we all end the same way.

Hand

When you've got a winning hand,
the cards fall in place.
You just have to play it out.

Game

No matter how bad the game,
you haven't lost
until the last card is played.

How

When tragedy strikes,
people say life must go on.
Don't say why or how.

Life

We come to life with nothing;
accumulate much.
Then we leave life with nothing.

No One

One by one, they go,
whether friend or foe.
No one is immune.

Story

Left heart at Stage Door Canteen.
Then shipped overseas.
Left life on the battle field.

Finally

Marched miles in mud, rain, snow;
could not do him in.
Many years later, age did.

Help

Retrorockets fired; no burn.
No burn; no return.
Houston, we've got a problem.

Taps

The bugler played taps slowly.
They lowered casket.
Soldier finally at peace now.

What'll You Have

Cracked an egg, ready to fry.
Small chick said, "Hold it!
Unless you want fried chicken!"

Live

We are but a blip
in the infinite time span.
Make the most of it.

Time

Is time an infinite thing?
Or is it finite?
We'll never know the answer.

Life

Like a candle that is snuffed,
thus can our life be.
So live it while you have it.

Above

General asked lone soldier,
"Where is your unit?"
"I think they're in heaven, Sir."

Spit Polish

Day of the Division parade,
creases, not wrinkles,
was the order of the day.

Motley

Jacket made here, pants there,
and the cap elsewhere.
You call this a *uni*form?

Together

Soldier cried when buddy died.
But ‘twas not for long.
Moments later, he joined him.

Work

No wonder we’re all tired.
Smiling’s less work than frowning,
but we’re all frowning.

Cheer

A smile can be real
or it can be false;
Only the smiler knows which.

Tears

Tears can be strange things.
They can mean sadness,
or they can mean happiness.

Lone

Marathoner finished race.
No one was around.
The race was yesterday.

Round

The Merry-go-round of fate
won't stop with one round.
It goes round and round, hang on.

Wait

Time and tide wait for no man.
If that is the case,
I won't wait for them either.

Watch

I have most accurate watch.
No, it does not run,
but twice every day, it's right.

Cycle

On eternal calendar,
Sun's pulse due this year.
Pack for move to Mars.

Full Moons

Mars is romantic planet.
Because has two moons,
there is always a full moon.

Well-Armed

Repairman wanted four arms.
Docs changed DNA
and now he has his four arms.

Morning

I looked in mirror.
I asked image, "Who are you?"
"I'm you," he replied.

Old

Had dispute with my clone.
He said, "You're dated.
You really must get hip, man."

A Game

We played at the game of life.
Won for many years.
But finally, life trumped us.

Ships

Tall sailing ships in harbor.
Sheets were fully set.
Bright sun reflected off sails.

Movies

What happened to the movies?
It's flash, crash and bang.
No more thought and no more plot.

Change

I’ve been wrong and I’ve been right.
Didn’t know it then,
but there’s no changing the past.

Remnant

I live on an asteroid.
It was a part of earth
till we blew it to pieces.

Save

Sent to a faraway land
to save the people.
Now it is in total ruin.

Cost

He asked me for a nickel
for a cup of coffee.
I asked him, “How old are you?”

The Way

You're getting nowhere in life.
Do you want success?
Learn to lie convincingly.

Lots

Get in politics, young man.
Billions for breakfast
and for lunch and for dinner.

Lift

Head man said, We have lift off.
Launch of a space probe?
No, lid from sim'ring soup pot.

Missing

The general told his men,
"Forearmed is well armed."
"Only have two arms," said one.

Companion

He's my constant companion,
but not when it's dark.
Who is he? He's my shadow.

What To Do

What is your mission in life?
Money, charity?
Think about it carefully.

Tongue Tied

It rolls off your tongue.
Just throw back your head and say,
Billion, billion, billion! Great!

Lore

Yet, with all of his vast lore,
why has not man learned
to peacefully coexist?

Learn

The teacher teaches,
but do the students learn?
Some do and some don't.

Message

A message in the sky asked,
"Who are the lonely?"
The answer is, "You and I."

Tick-tock

The clock of life ticks.
It can be wound but once,
so it will run down.

Alarm

When the clock of life alarms,
will you awaken
and heed it's warning to you.

Meaning

I read the poet's verses,
asked, "What do they mean?"
They mean what you want them to.

Master

He was master with keys.
He was a locksmith?
No, he was great pianist.

Worth

They say talk is cheap.
If it were worth anything,
we would all be rich.

Even Odds

I was fighting a duel.
Not so difficult.
Opponent had no weapon.

Where

Where's that thing called happiness?
I've waited lifelong.
Must come soon or it's too late.

Drifting

Like a ship without anchor,
or with no harbor,
drifting aimlessly through life.

Careful

This is a predatory world.
One preys on others.
So you have to watch yourself.

Misfortune

I think lady luck has died.
Never saw obit.
But haven't seen her, either.

Giving

Would give the shirt off his back.
He joined the Army.
He gave his country his life.

Change

What a difference a vowel makes.
Change a vowel, new word.
It’s pat, pet, pit, pot or put.

Race

You have run the race of life.
Winning or losing.
Does it really matter which?

Same

We are all the same.
We speak different languages.
That’s only difference.

Lifetime

Can a lifetime be a day?
On the other hand,
can a day be a lifetime?

Fresh

If life's not a winning hand,
can't throw in the cards.
You have to play the whole game.

Find

Ah! Too late we find
how so precious is a life.
Would it were sooner.

Cannot

You can take a life.
But you cannot restore it.
Act accordingly.

Not

Siren's like a lightning strike.
If you see or hear,
that one will not be for you.

Too Soon

They all died before their time.
But that was all right;
they died for their country.

Too Many

Millions died; for what?
We said, patriotic war.
That's what enemy said.

Ready

Are you ready, now,
for that last and final trip?
The clock has run out.

Soldiers

Tough solders are they.
Before, they were our children.
But now they have guns.

Mystery

Man! The paradox.
Spending millions to save lives;
the same to take lives.

Comparison

Some live in splendor;
some in abject poverty.
We need middle ground.

Great

Just when you're thinking
you are now going great guns,
your bullets run out.

Talk

If we could solve all our problems
just by our talking,
all those problems would be gone.

Mistake

He laid down prayer rug to pray.
Smart bomb hit wrong place.
Not even a thread was found.

Lower

The lamp of life burns lower.
Time is running out.
Make your peace with the world.

Laugh

Comedian told a joke.
It was so funny
that he could not stop laughing.

Helper

Lost in forest, driving snow;
met an arctic wolf.
She led me to a safe place.

Hello

Good morning! How do you do?
I’m Mister Haiku.
I come here to amuse you.

Difference

I heard a loud sigh.
Not of hopeless despair.
‘Twas reaper’s huge scythe.

Destination

Where is the next life?
When you see those gates of pearl,
you’ll wonder no more.

Time

Clocks in every room;
they each show a different time.
Wonder which is right.

Master

Time is our master.
We cannot turn it backward;
nor turn it forward.

Find

Turn back the pages of time
and what do you find?
Is it what you expected?

Why

If you live or die,
will anyone ever know
what's the reason why?

Memories

What are memories?
We recall the bygone past.
They're happy and sad.

Dreamer

I'm a daydreamer;
I'm also a night dreamer.
Nights OK. Days not.

Dream

I had a nightmare once.
You mean a bad dream?
No, my horse liked to ride, nights.

Pass

Time passes us by
and so does everything else.
In the end, nothing.

Play

If you have a winning hand,
it all falls into place.
You just have to keep playing.

Word

Killing, the buzzword today.
The words, "Thou shalt not"
seem to have been forgotten.

White

'Twas white and pristine.
Avalanche swept over all.
'Tis white and pristine.

Win

No matter how you play it,
you will lose the game
if it's not a winning hand.

Hope

You need cards for this hand?
You should be patient;
they'll come up in the next hand.

Endure

Darkness, light, sadness, joy.
All are part of life.
We must live through all of it.

Peace

Do not search for peace,
for you will find it nearby.
It is within you.

Burdens

Life's burdens many.
And life's burdens are heavy.
But we carry them.

Notice

A tri-folded flag.
Just compensation
for loss to family?

Ready

Life is passing by.
When the great reaper arrives,
will you be ready?

Past

What's so sad about the past?
Not there anymore,
and it never will be again.

Wrong

I thought everything went wrong.
But all those wrong things
turned out to be the right things.

Change

Some things in the past are sad.
And some are happy.
But it's done, can't change it now.

Reaper

The time of life is waning.
When that reaper comes,
will you be ready to go?

Crosses

In a field that's far away,
stand many crosses.
That's all there's left of our sons.

Over

What is done is done
and it cannot be undone,
so don't even try.

Done

Guns fire, bugle sounds.
A soldier is laid to rest.
All done, but for tears.

Day

Misty, dewy morn.
A new day is being born.
The earth to adorn.

Hear

Shot echoed down the valley.
Sniper lowered gun.
One man didn’t hear the shot.

Yes, No

Do you hear the shot that gets you?
Who knows the answer?
Certainly not the victim.

Sad

Disillusion, despair.
What has happened to our country?
Does anyone care?

Happy

Laugh and the world laughs with you.
Whoever said that,
the world is laughing at him.

Thinking

Things done or undone.
Your past deeds can haunt you.
Better to forget.

Name

First we learn to hate,
and then we learn to kill.
That's what they call war.

Rainbows

Chasing rainbows can be fun.
You'll never catch one.
No matter how hard you run.

Temp

Throw some coal on the fire;
it is freezing cold.
Where is that global warming?

Control

Whenever you think
you've got the world on a string,
becomes tiger's tail.

Where

Spaceman stopped on strange planet.
Asked what place is this.
We call it Earth, they answered.

Nowhere

Accelerated, blinding speed.
Four hundred horses.
Stopped at red light, next block.

Flames

Sitting around the fire
watching flickering flames
raises primeval instincts.

Orb

Oh, Mars! Red orb in the sky.
Will you welcome me,
if I come there bye and bye?

Heavy

The catastrophes,
like the sword of Damocles,
hang over my head.

Look

Closer than ever.
Power up observatory;
get good look at earth.

Moon

Circled moon's dark side.
Ancient civilization,
never seen before.

Red

We crossed the Mars red desert,
extending for miles,
then red meadows and forests.

Live

Sand and boulders red.
They think this planet is dead.
Not what natives said.

Shine

Looking up at Mars.
It outshines all of the stars.
Wonder if earth does.

Shining

Shining red and bright.
Not a flicker in the night.
Beautiful sight.

Better

Outshining all the stars
was the planet Mars.
'Twas red and magnificent.

Image

His best red image shone.
All the stars looked on.
Now Mars was in his glory.

Life

Is that what life is,
alternating grief and joy?
It is a rough ride.

Stopover

On the way to Jupiter,
Ion engines conked.
Stopped off on Mars for repairs.

Chase

Full moon chased Mars, east to west.
He never caught him.
Since never the twain shall meet.

Back

Eons ago, Mars came close.
Now it's here again.
Is this our time to return?

Orders

"Shoot first, ask questions later,"
was general's orders.
Shot by sentry late that night.

Wow

Beat a drum or blow a horn.
Make a lot a noise.
Let the world know all your joys.

Silence

Read a book last night.
Tube was strangely silent.
I should do that more often.

Look

Put on my glasses,
so I could see world better.
Should have left them off.

Improved

She was always the class clown;
made the lowest grades.
Now she's Madam President.

Misinfo

Patrol said all quiet,
so we advanced openly.
Most of the outfit wiped out.

Alert

Fire, murder, earthquake (scandal), storm.
'Twas the evening news.
Retired to my bomb shelter.

Books

I went down to the bookstore
and bought a new book.
Still haven't read the last one.

Maybe

Some day, some day, I muttered.
But then I forgot,
what I meant to do someday.

Lordy

Heaved a heavy sigh.
Yes, life can be difficult,
if you've no complaints.

Job

Submariner, flyer, slogger.
War's a dirty job.
No matter what you're doing.

Hold It

Tumbling down a mountainside,
passed surprised turtle.
"What's your hurry?" he asked.

Protection

Grizzly bears held convention.
Tax the Eskimos.
One fish per day from each.

Time

Listening to the classics
can be relaxing.
If you can wait long enough.

Penalty

If there were a penalty
for just killing time,
I'd be a serial killer.

Precious

More precious than gold is love.
It's not of this earth.
It comes from heaven above.

Passed

On my eightieth birthday,
where did the time go?
Seemed like only yesterday.

Mystery

What's it all about,
this mystery we call life?
But, more so, what's next?

Years

Where did it begin?
After years of joy and grief,
now where does it end?

Free

They say there is no free lunch.
Come to think of it,
no free breakfast or dinner.

Freeloaders

Picknickers left many crumbs.
So, that very night
ants had their own picnic.

Tough

Big elephant trumpeted.
Then the small mouse squeaked.
Elephant ran for his life.

Aliens

Aliens landed.
No antennae or big eyes.
Looked like my uncle.

Her

I once had a love.
But she's not here anymore.
I know she's above.

Story

Life is a diary.
We mean to write one story.
We write another.

Request

Sitting alone in corner.
A Princess approached;
"May I ask you to dance, Sir?"

Waltz

Orchestra played waltz.
Dancers glided around the floor.
Two never parted.

Name

When you haven't much to say,
you just write it down
and then call it a Haiku.

OK

If you feel bad a morning,
don't worry, you're OK.
If you feel heavenly, you're gone.

Reward

Attack success. General got
Medal of Honor.
Private got a small stone cross.

Survivors

Charged the hill, one man made it.
One foe left on top.
They eyed each other, shook hands.

Later

Kids playing in a sandbox.
Shovels and pails.
Now soldiers; guns and bayonets.

Talk

If loose lips can sink a ship,
that gabby jackass
will probably sink a whole fleet.

Proper

Here's how to drink wine.
Take your glass and sip slowly.
When it's all gone, quit.

Out

In his new world,
he was like a butterfly;
came out of cocoon.

Concern

"The people be damned.
It's party we care about,"
said politician.

True

If it sounds too good to be true,
you can be certain
it is too good to be true.

Hands

They're winning and losing hands.
If you lose or win,
will be up to the player.

Remember

We all have a golden age
that we remember.
When everything seemed so right.

Pot

Looking for that pot of gold
at the rainbow's end?
Don't bother; there is none there.

Gone

Don't look for the pot of gold
at the rainbow's end.
It was stolen years ago.

Ever

You will always be my love,
both here on this earth
and then in heaven above.

Need

Wind and water, those we need.
They are nature's gifts;
but not such great abundance.

Quiet

Sitting in church, so quiet,
free from the chaos
of an over-busy world.

Relief

I sought an interruption;
just a brief respite
from life's chaos and corruption.

Chance

Some are killed and some are spared.
Who knows which is which?
What will be our destiny?

Change

You can't change the past.
Maybe you can change present.
Who knows the future?

Stars

Oh! Twinkling stars in the sky!
How many are you?
I tried to count, but lost it.

Which

For every winner,
there is also a loser.
You can't be both.

Chief

Indian Chief gave a war whoop.
Was it an attack?
No, 'twas his birthday party.

Day

How far from nine to five?
It is a work day.
Sometimes seems like a lifetime.

Fate

Fortune comes to us in many forms.
So does misfortune.
We'll see both along life's path.

Music

Shouting and screaming.
What's that, they call it music?
It sounds more like noise.

Time

We have the future and the past.
Present never lasts.
It's either coming or going.

Game

Solitaire's a lonely game.
One consolation.
The cards don't argue with you.

Ten Hut

Sarge barked at his group,
and they all barked back at him.
He had K-9 crew.

Beach

Strolling on the beach,
waves crashing upon the shore.
Large gull swooped down.

Relics

Abandoned harbor.
Screeching gulls and rotting hulls.
Shades of yesteryear.

Careful

Man sweeping the shore
with a metal detector.
Boom! He was no more.

Slow

Traffic stopped for miles both ways.
Accident, flood, what?
A turtle crossing the road.

Depends

Living in the past
can be nice or can be sad.
It depends on you.

Early

First robin arrived.
The snow was still on the ground.
He said, "Spring is here."

Remains

Gulls and hulls are all that's left
of a once proud navy.
Even the sailors are gone.

Nothing

Except for the universe,
nothing's eternal.
Had no beginning or end.

Ideal

Fifteen, it was keen.
I'll never see it again.
It only happens once.

Fight

Life is a struggle,
no matter who you may be.
We each must fight it.

Surprise

Stared at him in disbelief.
"Who are you?" I asked.
"Your mirror image," he said.

Adrift

Planets live and planets die,
drifting through the sky.
Not for mortals to know why.

Planets

In the vast, dark universe,
planets formed, diverse.
Each was individual.

Forever

Silvery waves in the moonlight
wash upon the shore.
Now and forever, evermore.

The Way

It's a one way trip,
and, once you're on your way,
you cannot turn back.

What

Was no beginning,
no end, no middle.
Actually nothing.

Discourse

Conversation was extinct.
We each had hand holds.
Thus did we communicate.

Known

Confidentiality.
It's down the drain.
We spill our guts in public.

Talk

Heard guy on cell phone.
Rambling, rambling, rambling on.
Wondered when he'd stop.

Game

It's win, lose; lose, win.
What does it really matter?
It is just a game.

Talking

While playing solitaire,
I talked to my cards.
Only company I had.

Can Do

Can do the impossible.
Not by definition;
but who reads dictionaries.

Peace

Church is where you take your soul,
try to make life whole
in a world of chaos.

Go

In universe vast and dark,
a crew stood ready
on endless journey to embark.

All

Everything I have –
I owe it all to my wife.
She's now in heaven.

Write

Poets write from the soul.
Things that others never think.
Gifts to fellow man.

Flight

They flew overhead
in a perfect formation;
migrant flock of geese.

Language

Poets, those strange folk,
they speak in rhyme and meter.
Try to understand.

Look Out

The rain came down in buckets.
So many people hurt.
Yessir, those buckets are hard.

Promises

Politicians' promises.
Are they ever kept?
The answer must be, "Seldom."

Moon Shine

Full moon shone on high.
A spectacle in the sky.
A lonely wolf howled.

Hopes

Coins in a fountain,
pitched there by hopeful lovers.
Will their dreams come true?

Butterfly

Flutter by, Butterfly.
No artist could ever paint
the beauty of your wings.

Flutterby, Butterfly
on those wings so beautiful.
colors dazzling bright.

Flutter by, Butterfly.
Show those vivid colored wings
as long as you live.

Writer

What are you thinking about?
Whatever, write it.
Someone would like to read it.

Going

Over mountain, over stream;
he traveled with abandon.
A great Andean Condor.

Quatrain

Every night I greet
my friend shining ‘mong the stars.
The red planet Mars.

In that darkness vast
shining like a beacon bright.
The red planet Mars.

Tonight ‘twas raining.
So I could not greet my friend.
The red planet Mars.

Tomorrow I’ll look
once more in the sky for him.
The red planet Mars.

Babble

What language are they speaking
from tower of Babble,
and no one understands it?

News

The grief show ended.
The bad, sad news of the world,
told in a half hour.

No Show

Had date with lady luck.
She was late; I played.
She never came, I lost.

Red

Kings, Queens, Princes, Princesses.
Their blood is as red
as that of you and I.

Soldiers

We were all soldiers,
No matter what weapons,
no matter what flag.

Angels

Now up in heaven,
there are three new angels;
my wife and daughters.

Right

Would that I could right
all the wrong things I have done.
But it's too late now.

Remember

No, nothing lasts forever.
And, when it is gone,
be happy with what you had.

End

Large white flakes drift lazily down.
'Twas winter's last snow.
Blaze red cardinal flew by.

In Place

"It's heavier than a stone,"
he said with a groan.
So it's lain there hundred years.

Save

We try so hard to preserve
Civilization.
But there are so few of us.

Fight

"We will fight to the last man,"
said the general.
Gave all posthumous medals.

Winning

Every day more casualties.
They say we're winning.
I'm glad we aren't losing.

Play

You want to be musician?
Forget the piano.
Get a guitar and cowboy hat.

Thought

When I think of you,
I feel something strong within.
Wonder if it's love.

Shock

Like lightning to the rod,
so was my soul struck
by a look into your eyes.

Listen

Your conscience tells you what's right.
Should listen to it.
It's the guardian of your soul.

Gone

That empty feeling,
loneliness, it is gone now.
I have found a friend.

Yes

One day happy, next despair.
You are up then down.
Now you know you are in love.

Stop

All time has now stopped.
Every hour is like a day
when I'm not with you.

Near

Would there be a tear,
if I were no longer near?
It is "No," I fear.

Words

Sometimes words cannot express
what you feel inside.
Only you will ever know.

Viol

The strains of the violin,
the same as singing,
can touch your heart and soul.

Journey

We're whizzing through space.
Meteors, meteors, bang.
Oh well, you can't miss 'em all.

Wow

'Twas a spectacular sight.
What was it then?
I don't know, but it looked great.

You

If I hadn't you,
I'd taken trip to nowhere
and never come back.

Happy

I'm so happy I could cry.
All my cares, goodbye.
Since it is now you and I.

All

Every minute, hour, day,
Only think of you.
You have become my whole life.

Noblest

Noblest professions
have become glutinous pigs,
slopping at man's trough.

Contrast

Sweet hypocrisy!
We sing praises of ourselves,
but do evil deeds.

Us

Likes bring us together;
differences split us.
Which will overcome?

Gone

Can you live without a heart?
The Answer is, "Yes."
I lost mine and I'm still here.

Nine

Cloud Nine's here, hop on.
Take a ride to your dreams.
It's all in your mind.

Express

Last call, all aboard
for a heavenly journey.
On Cloud Nine express.

Pit

You have an empty feeling
in pit of stomach.
Don't worry, it's only love.

Ready

They are ghost armies.
And there are millions of them.
They're tired of waiting.

Must

This has to be love, because
I feel all these things.
Sorrows, sighs and dizzy spells.

Missing

Life without you is not living.
Something is missing.
And, yes, that something is you.

Answer

Talked to you incessantly,
always, in my thoughts.
I never got an answer.

Hearts

Two lonely hearts were so sad.
They met and were glad.
Those hearts, no longer lonely.

Try

Alone in a hostile world,
trying to survive
the twenty-first century.

Find

Happiness is in your mind,
not something you find.
It is with you all the time.

Enough

Just one kiss is not enough
from all of your charms.
I need much more of your love.

Life

A life without you?
It would not be a living;
merely existence.

Near

When I am near you,
my heart beats in double time.
When not; hardly beats.

Destiny

Destiny, you have now brought
love to empty life.
Pray, never take her away.

Songs

Sad songs aren't sad anymore.
Not since I met you.
Every song's a happy song.

Talk

I've heard talk is cheap.
But when I got my phone bill,
it was expensive.

Beat

Like two hearts that beat as one,
so did our hearts beat.
Will it always be that way?

Fast

How fast can it take
for two souls to fall in love?
Faster than lightning!

Pain

Yes, the pain of love can hurt.
On the other hand,
love's pain can be very sweet.

Power

There is a power
that's able to conquer all.
It's the power of love.

Love

Love started with a spark,
became a conflagration.
We're consumed by love.

When / Life

My life is just a huge sigh.
Joy passes me by.
When will happiness arrive?

Books

Books can be your friends.
They can also be your foes.
You're the only one who knows.

Mind / Off or On

My mind is turned off today.
No useful thoughts there.
I'll turn it on tomorrow.

Coffee

He asked me for a nickel
for cup of coffee.
I asked how old are you?

Common

What do they have in common,
Spies, politicians?
They're both accomplished liars.

Blow

You can't keep a lid
on top of a boiling pot.
It's going to blow.

Star

Looking at a star,
Wondering if there you are;
or are you now dead?

Dimensions

Lived in third dimension; bored.
Tried two; that was flat.
Next, will try fourth dimension.

History

So first, who were you?
And presently, who are you?
Then, who will you be?

Guide

Full moon, shine on high.
Like a beacon in the sky.
Guide me to my love.

Friend

Bad dreams, thoughts and days;
All of them, things of the past.
Now I have a friend.

Funny

“Know any new jokes?” friend asked.
Told a funny joke;
so funny that he died laughing.

Time

Time! The paradox.
It will always be with us.
But it's also gone.

Bombs

How many must die,
and how many more must cry?
End Death from the sky.

Morning Fog

It's early morning
and my body is awake,
but my mind is asleep.

The News

If watching the news
gives you nothing but the blues,
well then, take a snooze.

Nature

The beauty of nature
is put there for all to see.
Just open your eyes!

Waste

Watching the traffic go by,
almost had to cry
at the waste of earth's treasures.

Novel

I started writing.
My hands moved furiously.
Result, finished novel.

Walking/Talking

I walk through my house,
always talking to myself;
there's no one else here.

Life

Life is but a frustration.
Morning, noon and night.
Will it ever be easy?

Tell Me

Do you know what happiness is?
If you do tell me.
'Cause I know only sadness.

Peanuts

I ate one peanut.
I couldn't stop eating them.
I ate the whole can.

Win

Play the lottery.
You'll make a contribution
to the one who wins.

Dance

"May I have this dance?"
The Earth said to the Moon.
"'Twill be eternal."

Mirror

I looked into the mirror
and what did I see?
My soul staring back at me.

Trip

That other world.
Is it? If so, where is it?
When will I go there?

Master

Master of his Universe,
looking down on all,
the eagle soared endlessly.

Lists

Every day I make
a long list of things to do,
which I'll never do.

Philosophy

I am a philosopher.
I look for answers
to things that have no answers.

Think

I'm working for a think tank.
There's lots of thinking,
but never any action.

Nature

Nature can be cruel.
Just ask any of those fools
who dare to oppose her.

Wing

Fame, you fleeting thing.
For time you landed on me.
And then you took wing.

Light

My candle blew out.
So now I won't be able
to find honest man.

Form

To fill out a form,
you have to fill in the blanks.
That's all there is, thanks.

Doom

Chaos and catastrophe
have become the rule
in an avaricious world.

Storm

The sun hid behind the clouds.
We never found him.
Storm, lightning, rain in torrents.

When

Tell me, what is time?
Can you see, feel, hear, smell it?
Don't have an answer.

Clouds

Puffy clouds float by.
Making patterns in the sky.
Ne'er again the same.

Over

You can go over rainbow.
Just climb to the top.
Downhill slide will be easy.

Coming

Frost on the mountain top.
Dew in the valley.
The spring flowers are sprouting.

Diet

You have got me doing things
I never did before
I now eat asparagus

Perfect

We fit together
Like jig-saw puzzle pieces.
We're a perfect match.

Moon

Blue moon, silver moon
No matter what your color
You are beautiful

Everything

What is perfection?
Voice like music, eyes like stars
A smile like sunshine

Enclosed

In his own world
He lived most contentedly
He's still living there

Change

The shadows of time –
They can be long or be short;
You cannot change it.

Where

What happened to family?
What happened to home?
Both are gone for those who roam.

Attention

Sire, the people are restless.
Oh! Then start a war!
That will get their attention.

Trip

How do you get to the moon?
Just contact the man,
And he'll give you directions

More

His pockets empty;
But he was well and happy.
Couldn't ask for more.

Choir

Humming birds hummed soprano.
Song birds sang alto.
And the pond frogs croaked the bass.

What

Envy the ostrich.
He sticks his head in the sand.
Let's the world go by.

Art

Art takes many forms.
Music, poetry, literature.
Do we appreciate?

Communicate

I wish that my brain
would inform all my muscles
that they are not tired.

Sync

Mind and body are not in sync.
Mind says I'm fifteen,
but my body says eighty.

Entertainment

The choral group sang,
the orchestra played along,
and I went to sleep.

Returned

All his battles were over;
the soldier came home.
At least, a part of him did.

Benefactors

We who came back home
owe our mortal existence
to those who did not.

Gone

Enjoyed his last days on earth.
So he is dead now?
No, he’s living on the moon.

Long

So how long is forever?
Do you want to know?
Just wait around to find out.

Quick

Blink your eye and life goes by.
What happened to it?
Tomorrow's now yesterday.

Life

Is life so miserable?
Is it all so sad?
Why can't I think happy thoughts?

Going

Going nowhere fast,
I finally arrived at last
Where was it? Nowhere!

Emigration

Getting warm again.
It's time for us to pack up
and return to Mars.

Boot

He was a boot on the ground.
Fought for his country.
Now he's a boot in the ground.

Forgot

Extended my term.
Two more months, but they forgot
to extend my life.

Always

I was a soldier,
and now I always will be;
through eternity.

Wait

What you would do tomorrow
will never get done,
'cause tomorrow never comes.

Fame

Fame's a fleeting thing.
Today everyone knows you.
Tomorrow no one.

Change

Puffy clouds float by
Showing shapes ne'er seen before
And ne'er seen again.

Same

Travel the world and you will see;
other people
are just the same as you and me.

Tarry

Something you don't want to do.
Do it tomorrow.
'Cause tomorrow never comes.

Rain

How many rain drops falling?
Really want to know?
Just ask any friendly duck.

Direction

Birds flying south, it's Autumn.
Flying north, it's spring.
What if they go east or west?

Surprise

Skier saw a tree.
Right foot went right, left foot left.
The result was "Ouch!"

Walls

If the walls could talk,
how do you think they would be?
Concrete or discrete?

Avoid

We are all shunners.
Combination, adoration.
Name it, we shun it.

The Fray

Astride mighty steed,
rode bravely into the fray.
Never rode away.

Love

Love can be happy;
but it can also be sad.
You have to take both.

Letters

Love letters in the sand.
Thoughts that would last forever.
Washed out by the next tide.

Problem

They have a crisis
down at the crisis center.
There are no crises.

Together

War and heroics;
they always go together.
So do war and death.

Hello

Nature's alarm clock
broke the sun's nightly slumber.
"Good morning," he said.

Chance

The ticker ticked, shouts rang out.
Bids were asked and made.
My money went down the drain.

Fragile

Fragile as a flower.
Or wings of a butterfly.
Just as beautiful.

Name

The bullet with your name on.
How can you dodge it?
You can try changing your name

Master

Mother Nature and Father Time
are hard task masters.
You'd best obey their biddings.

Perishable

Empires rise and empires fall.
None last forever.
Here today, gone tomorrow.

Songs

Old songs can bring back
memories of things long ago,
both happy and sad.

Unknown

What is beyond us?
So, when you know the answer,
you can tell no one.

Meeting

So, will our souls meet
in some mistier beyond?
Freed from worldly bonds?

Save

Sin will save the world,
so the politicians say.
If so, we're well on the way.

Life

Yesterday you were unknown.
Today you're famous.
Tomorrow you're history.

Name

If you haven't much to say.
you just write it down.
And then call it a Haiku.

Live

Writing Haiku
is not nearly as much fun
as living Haiku.

Speak

Have you lots to say?
But you have not many words.
Then write a Haiku.

Trash

On time's huge trash heap,
we toss yesterday's treasures.
Nobody cares now.

Comrades

Cradled in his arms
he held a fellow soldier.
Both of them shed tears.

Ache

My back is aching.
Do you have a malady?
No, someone stabbed me.

Sin

So what is a sin?
Is it when the deed does end?
Or when it begins?

Money

Money won't hug you.
Won't comfort you when you're sad.
Is that what you want?

Gone

Like windblown blossoms,
my lifelong aspirations
vanished before me.

Battle

Who will get my soul?
It's been a lifelong struggle
twixt good and evil.

Past

I often wonder.
What happened to yesteryear?
Where has it gone?

Forever

Full moon shone on high.
'Twas shining for you and I.
It will until I die.

Gate

What is a gate for?
Is it to allow entry
or to prevent it?

Progress

The present becomes the past.
Future the present.
Never ending procession.

Duty

Our job is killing.
That's because we are soldiers;
and also dying.

Fright

The thunder rumbled loudly.
Bolt of lightning struck.
A field mouse ran for cover.

Nice

Something's unpleasant?
Well, you give a nice name,
then just forget it.

Confused

My life is a mess.
Half of me is here, half there.
Don't know which is which.

Problems

I'm an emotional wreck.
Can't help being sad
and can't help being happy.

Together

We were friends for life.
In both good times and in strife.
And she was my wife.

Eyes

Eyes across the table,
looking deep into the soul.
'Twas love at first sight.

Duty

Soldier took dead aim,
asked the Lord for forgiveness,
then pulled the trigger.

Past

You long for what's past.
It is not there anymore.
Forget about it.

Difference

What's the difference
between an ache and a pain?
It's a groan or moan.

CPSIA information can be obtained
at www.ICGtesting.com
Printed in the USA
FFOW01n1546100314
4127FF

9 781618 637178